Rita F. Snowden is wi
is the author of more ~~~~ ~~~~, ~~~~ books for adults and
children. After six years in business she trained as a
deaconess of the New Zealand Methodist Church, serving
in turn two pioneer country areas before moving to the
largest city for several years of social work during an
economic depression.

Miss Snowden has served the world Church, beyond
her own denomination, with regular broadcasting commit-
ments. She has written and spoken in Britain, Canada, the
United States, in Australia, and in Tonga at the invitation
of Queen Salote. She has represented her church at the
World Methodist Conference in Oxford; later being
elected the first woman Vice-President of the New
Zealand Methodist Church, and President of its Deaconess Association. She is an Honorary Vice-President of the
New Zealand Women Writers' Society, a Fellow of the
International Institute of Arts and Letters, and a member
of P.E.N.

Miss Snowden has been honoured by the award of the
Order of the British Empire, and by the citation of 'The
Upper Room' in America.

Her most recent books are *Prayers for Busy People*,
Christianity Close to Life, *Bedtime Stories and Prayers*
(for children), *I Believe Here and Now*, and *Discoveries
that Delight*.

Books by the same author
available in Fount Paperbacks

BEDTIME STORIES AND PRAYERS
(for children)
CHRISTIANITY CLOSE TO LIFE
DISCOVERIES THAT DELIGHT
I BELIEVE HERE AND NOW
MORE PRAYERS FOR WOMEN
PRAYERS FOR BUSY PEOPLE
PRAYERS FOR THE FAMILY
PRAYERS IN LATER LIFE
A WOMAN'S BOOK OF PRAYERS

Rita Snowden also edited
IN THE HANDS OF GOD
by William Barclay

RITA F. SNOWDEN

FURTHER GOOD NEWS

Collins
FOUNT PAPERBACKS

First published by Fount Paperbacks, London in 1983

© 1983 by Rita F. Snowden

Made and printed in Great Britain by
William Collins Sons & Co Ltd, Glasgow

Reaching out to my friend
in Boston, U.S.A.,
Leonida —
Mrs Loring Conant

Contents

Introduction

Are you constantly eager for 'Good News'? I am. And I believe God is, too.

This, we discover, is a world where good happenings mingle with bad – where tiny ones suffer sickness, teen-agers know cruelty, young men and women engage in drink or drugs; where many marriages entered upon in hope, collapse, old people are robbed of slender savings, and desperate refugees have to escape from war zones in leaky boats, or trudge miles with pitiful little bundles on their backs.

Some Good News that might be shared, alas, is not even noticed. Many reporters in training are not, it seems, taught to search for it – their interest is rather in things 'shocking' that will make headlines – and that makes the evaluation of one's daily newspaper often depressing. Dr Micklem, Principal of Mansfield College, Oxford, felt this shape of things that we share, to be no new tendency. 'Had there been a news agency like Reuters in the first century A.D.,' he said, 'it is doubtful whether the conversion of Paul on the Damascus Road – that soon shook the world – would have made a headline!'

And all the while, moving amongst men and women, there are happenings that lift the heart. I have discovered this since I have daily doings with people who build good homes, and rejoice in their families; who garden eagerly, and give away a generous part of what they grow; people, ordinary enough, who rise early, and work hard, who laugh, and make music; who play games, and read books from the world's riches; and who never fail to fling a compassionate arm round the shoulder of a suffering neighbour. Many of these also make time in their lives for worship.

Our newspapers tell us dolefully of 'the generation gap'. But present today in many places, it is only half the story. In my morning paper lately came to me news of a kind that I can only describe as 'Good'. It rejoiced my heart; and I'm sure it did God's heart, too. I read and re-read of Mrs Gwladys Ann Tudor, moving constantly amongst the young, though she is not herself young any more. Life has cost her a good deal of effort to get to this coveted point, whilst tending two antique shops. Her chief concern, meanwhile, is as a University student, a graduate who that very week had been called to the Capping ceremony in our Town Hall. Her only care was that she might not hear her name called since, as she confessed to the reporter who gleaned for me her story, she is deaf, *and eighty-two*!

Yet her studies had been a glorious exercise in sharing – the young with whom she had spent her days at study had been so very co-operative. And at day's end, she had carried home a tape recorder to play back to herself at night the lectures given that day. From time to time, her fellow students had invited her to their parties. 'I haven't always gone', she had to admit, 'because I can't properly hear what anyone is saying. Though', pausing, 'I did go to our class break-up!'

'Last year,' my newspaper was able to add, 'Mrs Tudor and a member of her family whom she calls "my young sister" – a seventy-year-old – went on a safari up the Amazon River. There, she was able to study at close quarters an Indian tribe that had interested her during the previous year. While other people of Mrs Tudor's age', added the reporter, 'have retired behind their knitting, Mrs Tudor is busily looking around.'

Throughout her university studies, this grand old soul refused to recognize what is glibly referred to as *the generation gap.* Amidst much in the paper that was dispiriting, this was Good News.

Sometimes it is the mail, I find, that brings me News that I am glad to receive. As an author of many books, it is my constant joy to receive letters from unknown readers, many of them living far from my little home country of New Zealand, down at the bottom of the globe. Added to the Good News that came to me through my letterbox lately was Further Good News. One such reader wrote: 'I live *within the Arctic Circle.* My work is among mentally retarded people. They are fine people in many ways.' Then, this appreciative reader went on to tell me of their little church, finishing with Christian greetings, adding to her signature, the postscript: 'Come and see me if ever you are this way.' (Surely, my most remote reader! The wonder is that within our hearts – despite differences of geography, and much else, is this wonderful sharing of deep-down things that matter!) I like to think that I might some day get to Borkenes – up at the top of this old world.

Language, of course, is sometimes a difficulty, although translations help. Lately, I received from the publishers one book in Finnish, one in German, and one in Japanese. This is Further Good News to any author, added to the original English in which a book appears. The day after the post brought me copies of my Japanese translation, I was in the wash-room of our City Library, and there was a woman who beamed at me as I entered. I did not know her, but felt she must surely be a member of some gathering I had addressed some time, somewhere. She turned out to be the wife of a Presbyterian minister with whom I'd had dealings fifteen years or so ago. I asked her about their family – ages and interests – and she asked me about mine: my 'family of books'. I told her that the number had grown, and now includes some in Braille, in Talking Books, and in translation. 'Only yesterday,' I

11

added brightly, 'I received copies of the Japanese one.'
'How interesting!' she exclaimed. 'As a matter of fact,
we've a little Japanese lady in our congregation. I'm not
at all sure what she makes of us, she has so little English;
but she has two children who come to our Sunday School
– they go to day school too, of course.'

I replied: 'Well, the publishers have sent me three
copies of my book in Japanese. If you'll be good enough
to give me your address, I'll send her one, care of your
letterbox.' And this was done.

A day or so later, I received a letter, on behalf of the
Japanese mother: 'Thank you for the little book *in my own
language, in a foreign land!*'

Lately came a letter to my postbox from Nigeria,
addressed in bold capital letters but with a surprising
curiosity, which told me at once that its writer was not
familiar with my language. It was from a teenage student,
who began: 'I must not let myself enjoy your books any
more without saying, "Thank-you!" I plan to be a lawyer
some day.' Then he went on to tell me of his church, and
his family. But it was his envelope which brought a
chuckle: RITA SNOWDEN, AUTHOR OF GOOD
BOOKS. Then, at a loss to know how to deal with my
O.B.E., he added, in letters as bold: (IN ROYALTY).

I have a pile of such letters from readers, and when they
bring me, in addition to news of their reading, news of
their church, Further Good News is added.

I like the expectation of the old church custodian of
whom Dr Roy Smith tells. Returning from an extended
journey, the old fellow met him one morning with the
question: 'Good morning, Doctor! *Do you bring any late
news from God, this morning?*' (Any 'late news', meaning
recent news, further news, anything of a spiritual kind.)

Dr David Read – the preaching minister and author of
a number of loved books on my shelves – whom I'd heard
in his own pulpit in Madison Avenue Presbyterian

Church, New York, loved to say plainly: '*Jesus Christ is Good News!* All who yielded their lives to Him, from the earliest days, to the present moment, know this is true.' He came into our world, as related in the pages of the gospels, beginning in Bethlehem – but the reality of His presence does not end there. He came as a Babe; but He has not remained a Babe. Limited to reaching a relatively small number during His human earth-life, as Story-teller, Teacher, Healer, Saviour, He is now Risen from the Dead, available ever more.

Some in our midst who have been to Sunday School in childhood; some young men and women who have attended Bible Class; some mature folk who have found themselves in church a few times, for weddings, baptisms, and funerals, are inclined to think that when it comes to religion, *they know it all*. But this is a pathetic notion. Not only is there Good News to be had, through the redeeming, risen power of Christ – but all the time, as life goes on, Further Good News. We none of us know it all!

Dr J.S. Stewart, beloved Scottish preacher and writer, throws out to us a lively challenge: 'It is an awful thing,' says he, 'to hear Christians, as I have heard them, bemoaning as pessimistically as any unbeliever. Do let us believe our own Faith, that the God Who came . . . through the thick darkness of Calvary, is not deserting the world stumbling through these shadows now. The basic fact of history is not the iron curtain, but the rent veil; not the devil's strategy, but the Divine sovereignty. *Sursum corda* – lift up your hearts!' I can say – with Christ –

> *This is my Father's world,*
> And to my listening ears,
> All Nature sings, and round me rings
> The music of the spheres.

Further Good News

This is my Father's world.
I rest me in the thought
Of rocks and trees, of skies and seas:
His hand the wonders wrought.

This is my Father's world,
O! let me ne'er forget
That though the wrong seems oft so strong,
God is the Ruler yet!

(Maltbie Badcock)

Good News – of Fingertips

I was fascinated. Nothing of the sort had ever happened to me before. I had been some months in London and the time had come to return home, halfway round the world, by way of America. My flight papers had been given attention, but it now seemed that I couldn't begin that journey without a final check.

Fingerprints, of course, as a system of identification, were very ancient. An early king, unable to sign his name, was able to satisfy a demand by printing down one of his thumbs smudged with dye. It was later understood that such a pattern, resulting from the minute ridges on thumbs and fingers, differed with each individual – and with each finger – even for the newly-born.

So I was pleased to comply with the American office request in London, and have my fingerprints filed. (This fascinating physiological fact, once recognized, had been early worked into a system for persons wanted for wrongdoing; and, in time, extended to take in travel requirements.)

There is nothing so individual – unless it's Love. And there is no forgetting the old saying: *Love has an individualizing effect.* One sees it clearly in the content of the parables of our Lord: that of the *one* son; the *one* coin; the *one* sheep (Luke 15:3–32; AV).

It is all too easy in these crowded, casual times, to see people as statistics; it is common to refer to fellow workers as 'personnel'; airlines refer to travellers as 'seats'; hotels call them 'beds' – all things capable of manipulation. Others refer to those who ride into the city with them as 'strap-hangers' – they are never 'persons', individuals, with unique characteristics.

And all the time, in reality, they are more than 'digits' in a census-taking; more than 'types', 'age groups'. One by one, our approach to them must reach up to the evaluation of our Lord. 'One by one,' as the Bishop of the great city of Birmingham put it, 'good men of the Establishment came to Him secretly by night; people whom the world rejected, came to Him openly by day.'

Writing also during our century, to suffering Katherine Mansfield the story-teller, D.H. Lawrence showed himself completely off the beam: 'Cheer up, Kate, Jesus is a back number!'

He never was; He *led* His young followers, men and women, across the field paths from place to place; and He led them into lasting ideas and values. And He does still – *not least in the value of each person.* It is a wonderful thing that here and there amongst us are countless men and women who grasp this today. It reveals itself in reverence for personality: in sickness and in health, in childhood, youth, and old age. One of our city's honoured doctors, some time ago, took pains to underline this essential, and it reached me as the best piece of news in my paper that particular morning. (I cut it out, so that I might share it.) 'The danger', said he, 'of looking on a patient as "a specimen" that goes with a large sheaf of notes, is one that will have to be faced and overcome. Imagine a modern surgeon', he added, 'hurrying down the road from Jerusalem, to give a paper at the Jericho Medical Association, excusing himself for not stopping to help a man who had fallen among thieves – even if the subject of his paper was to be "The treatment of shock, and multiple injuries."'

This New Testament story of the Good Samaritan – *the Supreme Story-teller's expression of God's values* – lasts on. In this earthly experience we cannot, of course, fully know each of our fellows – but each, nevertheless, is gifted with a set of fingerprints indicative of his or her own personality, his or her own eternal worth. The significance of fingertips, in terms of individuality, remains, whoever we are, wherever we are. I remember how clearly this was made known to me during a long day, not far from Buckingham Palace, at a Coronation Celebration. We were seated there under the sky as that day dawned, hundreds and thousands of us, faces, faces, faces. And not one would I have mistaken for my friend! Two eyes, a nose and a mouth each – and yet individual. So wonderful is the creativeness of God!

I link it now with this more recent occasion in London – when getting my fingerprints recorded. Somewhere, this moment, in the multitudinous files of America, I suppose, they are purposefully kept. I was fascinated to read of a like experience in Ann Bridge's book *Facts and Fiction*. When told that she must present herself for fingerprinting, as a certain hour approached, she exclaimed: 'Oh, shall I really? How lovely!' Being fingerprinted, she commented, was an experience, 'like pulling the communication cord in a train; something that I had always longed for, hitherto in vain.' (Then she had to add what I find I have myself left out: 'I must say the black took a lot of getting off.')

Someone has drawn our attention to the fact that there are three attitudes that can be adopted in this life – *towards* people; *away* from people; and *against* people. This is a three-fold truth, that families, priests, parsons, teachers and students, officers of trade-unions, and labourers have to decide on. God-the-Father's individualizing Love is never in question, repeated in the Earth-life of our young Lord and Master.

> Sea folk were His, He knew the lash
>   Of whirling sea;

He knew the drag of empty nets
   On Galilee.

Hill folk were His, He knew the bells
   Of sheep at night;
He knew the peace that souls may find
   On starlit height.

Town folk were His, He knew the need
   Of poor and proud;
He found that man might walk alone
   Within a crowd.

All folk are His, He knows the way—
   Each rut and stone;
He moves beside us so that none
   Need climb alone!

(Unknown)

Good News – of Creation

I look at my hands – making gardens, making paintings, pieces of pottery, puddings, and pretty vases of flowers – and know them to be among life's greatest wonders. Is this what an early Bible verse means? 'God said, Let us make man in our image, after our likeness ... So God created man in his own image, in the image of God created he him' (Genesis 1:26–27; A.V.). Does this mean that the Creator was *making His creation a creator, too*? I think so, whatever else it means.

Certainly this world in which we live came to us from the hands of God. The versifier who thought, and wrote, otherwise can now only be counted far off the mark. Said he:

> The earth's a lot of dust,
> The sky's a lot of air,
> The sea's a lot of water
> That just happened to be there.

But there is nothing in the Bible as vague as that concerning the creation of our earth, however we think it happened, in a brief six days of Time, with the Creator resting on the seventh; or slowly, purposefully evolving through many centuries. Whatever the method, behind this marvellous happening, stood *God the Creator*!

Dr Harry Fosdick, beloved preacher and writer of our day, enlarging on this approach, very tellingly says: 'To suppose that physical particles manoeuvring in the void fortuitously arranged themselves into planets, forests, mothers, musicians, artists, poets, scientists, and saints, is not to work out a philosophy; it is to run away from philosophy and believe in magic.'

One of the noble prayers that you and I can offer to God in this life is: 'Creator, make me creative. Don't let me sit on my hands idly. Make me willing to use my mind, my imagination, my hands.' My dear friend from Boston, U.S.A., has received her answer to this prayer: and we talked about it, when she visited us the other day. When her two grown children, part of a family all musical, gave her a present, some time before her visit, they selected a harpsichord kit. 'Their love at that time, when my husband had just gone on his longest journey,' said she, 'not only sustained me, but added interest to my days.'

Then she went on to tell me about the creation of the instrument itself. I was very interested; I had never heard of a lay person achieving such. Certainly, my friend was musical; certainly, her two young people suggested that she should go to the Eric Hertz workshop to see a finished product. This she did; and two weeks later, her own kit arrived.

'I had studied the inch-thick book of directions carefully,' she added, 'firstly counting every item as listed, to make sure that all were present. Not one – a screw, nail, pin, wire, felt, key, piece of sandpaper – was missing. Nor glue, nor eight parts of each of the 114 jacks.'

Then she went on to tell how she 'created' the whole. 'First,' said she, 'I sanded the three legs, with three different grades of sandpaper, then finished them with a mixture of half-and-half boiled linseed oil and turpentine. Then I screwed them into the empty frame, and placed it on its feet.

'It took about three weeks for the keyboard preparation, and six weeks to assemble the jacks; and a further six weeks to design and paint the soundboard. Then days were spent sanding the entire case, including the lid. [Everything was cherry, except the soundboard, which was of very thin spruce.] The alignment of the strings and slots for the jacks was one of the most difficult procedures, the other being the accurate placing of the soundboard. The final touch was the stringing – and when it was completed, and I touched the keys', she added, her eyes lighting up with the true creator's joy, 'and heard my first note, *it was like hearing one's baby's first cry!*'

To register this glorious event in the life of all of them, my friend's son took a picture of her harpsichord, in her dining room, and later presented her with a series of pictures to mark the experience. The title he had chosen for the set was, tellingly enough, 'The Creation'.

My friend's father was very musical, she was glad to tell me, 'playing the piano to me every night; as I did later, for my two children when they were young. And now their families are reaping a music harvest – my daughter's three sons play, between them, the cello, clarinet, saxophone, trumpet, bass horn, trombone, french horn, piano, organ, and they all, including father and mother, play recorders. My son plays the violin, as well as the piano and recorder; his daughter, the piano and recorder; and his son, the oboe as well as the recorder,' she was happy to add. 'But the highest moment for me – as you will understand – was when, six years ago, I "created" my harpsichord!'

Had anyone noticed, as we sat together in our home talking, they must have observed how my face lit up, too. For it is always a wonderful thing to have the privilege of hearing of another's 'creation'. My friend's *prayer* – whatever her actual words, and however often spoken – was answered. I know, deep down in my heart, what that means to my friend, for I, too, have 'created' books, addresses, and many other things, besides those listed at the beginning of this fascinating chapter.

I remember to this day the thrill which came to me when I realized that God had not only once created *but is always creating!* And that I may continue to be a 'creator', too.

Season by season it happens; day and night. Often the words of another rise to my lips, in the hush of night, out of doors:

> *Creator of the countless stars*
> *That fill the Milky Way,*
> *I trembling stand before Thy might*
> *And know not how to pray.*

But pray I must, somehow, if I am to reach my fullest expression as a person 'created in God's image'. I am, of course, dependent for this on the endless, enabling power of 'The Great Creator Himself'. I like the way Dr L.P. Jacks puts it, and take the liberty of copying out his words. I want – every bit as much as Dr Jacks himself – to be 'a creator'. That, I believe, is to reach my full potential in this wonderful world in which He has set me. So I take Dr Jacks' striking words upon my lips, again and again: 'In Whom do I live, and move, and have my being? In Him. Whose the vitality of the air I draw in with every breath? His. Whose the pressure of the atmosphere, fifteen pounds avoirdupois to every square inch of my body? His. Whose the first support of the ground under my feet and the light of consciousness wherewith I am conscious of it? His. In Whose light do I see what is visible, in Whose sound hear what is audible, in Whose strength do what is doable? In His. Who keeps my heart beating from moment to moment, and the blood coursing through my veins? He Who keeps the earth spinning on its axis, the fires burning in the sun, and Orion on his stately march amid the constellations; He Who paves the Milky Way with millions of worlds. *Awful thoughts ... and tremendous facts!*'

So, I pause, to remember my ongoing course as 'a creator'! I have no little children to whom I can impart this wonderful possibility – sometimes I wish I had, but I am told that it is not an easy undertaking, in this modern setting in which our life is lived today. That's a pity! Frances Wilkinson, in her little family book, *Growing Up in Christ*, S.C.M. Press, says: 'There is a special responsibility laid on those of us who bring up our children in towns. The idea of God as Creator is not so easily passed on when so much of our environment is man-made and unlovely. The sight of a strawberry to a town child does not call up the memory of the silvery dew on the leaves, the feel of gossamer on the cheek, and the curling wispy mist of early morning. It is more likely to remind him of shops and money, "punnets" and chips, and mother saying they are expensive.' This is a loss, in growing up and when one is grown up. We cannot manage at all without the Creator – or without, in the situation in which He has set us, *being creative*!

Good News – concerning Our Senses

I can't now remember how young or trying I was when I first heard my parents and teachers say: 'Now use your senses!' But those simple words had a forbidding sound about them, which was a pity. For, taken even in their literal sense, they are some of the most glorious words in the world! During the whole of one's life there is seldom an adventure to compare with *using one's senses*.

> For quite small children—
> each morning brings a world of their
>   own making,
> with colours scarcely dry,
> created at the moment of awaking,
> *by ear and hand and eye.*

I like the mood of that unknown writer's words, although they are limited. He seems to suggest that childish senses are but *three*. But, of course, they are not.

Geoffrey Peachy moves nearer to the truth, in his glad hymn, with each of *four* verses giving thanks for one sense: Sight, Touch, Speech, Hearing. It begins:

> O God our Father, Who has sent
>   The gift of *sight* that we might know
> The glories of Thy firmament,
>   The beauty of the earth below;
> *For this great gift, O Lord, we raise*
> *Our song in gratitude and praise.*

> O Christ, Who by Thy *touch*, repaired
>   The loss of him deprived of sound,

Good News – concerning Our Senses

We offer thanks for hearing spared,
   For all the joys in music found;
For this great gift, O Christ, we raise
Our song in gratitude and praise.

O Spirit Who, in tongues of flame,
   With many *tongues* the saints endowed,
We magnify Thy Holy Name
   That we can tell our thoughts aloud;
For this great gift, O Lord, we raise
Our song of gratitude and praise.

We pray that muted tongues may voice
   The praises of our God and King,
That ears, untuned to sound, rejoice
   To *hear* the Word Thy angels bring;
And sightless eyes Thy glory see,
   O Blessed, Holy Trinity.

(Geoffrey Peachy)

Sight is a sense that many would put first – lovers of gardens, countrysides and coastlines. Instructors in art are at pains to tell us, set on reproducing and interpreting these generous gifts of God, that every twenty minutes the light changes. John Constable, speaking of that bit of England that he made world-famous around his beloved Flatford Mill, and which I have been privileged to visit, rejoiced to say: 'No two days are alike, nor even two hours, neither two leaves of a tree alike, since the creation of the world.'

It would be presumptuous for me, as a passing dweller among these lovely things, with much to learn, to suggest that the Burning Bush, at the back of the desert, when the world was young, only burned because Moses the shepherd looked. I don't know – I can't know. But I do know with a measure of certainty that much that is as transforming in the spirit of a man can be lost for ever, if he doesn't look – and the same, of course, is true of a woman!

One day, I found myself sharing a like experience to that known by Moses in the desert, in the place where I live, and in these modern times. I've never forgotten the glory of it. I felt moved to call it 'Autumn Vision', beginning with a question:

> What shall I do?
> The tall poplar at street's end
> Is a living shock of fire,
> a shaft golden, unconsumed
> as the burning bush
> in the desert of the shepherd
> who took the shoes from off his feet.

> (R.F.S.)

'Christianity...' one of our modern writers, whose sensitivity has taught me much in my growing up says, 'does not teach that you get nearer to God by getting away from sense and things; it does not despise matter, *it consecrates it*.' Christians are encouraged to acknowledge *Sight* as one of God's very greatest gifts. One of our fellow believers, away back in Sarum, in 1558, knew that, and fashioned that lovely little prayer-hymn that we still sing:

> God be in my head,
> And in my understanding—

> *God be in my eyes,*
> *And in my looking.*

And added to these are other petitions as relevant, as simple. In early times – three or four centuries ago, when men and women first began to sing it – it carried no more significance than it does today. Nor does geography count – be it in the sacred community of Sarum, in the south of England, or in the traffic-echoing street where I live, behind my little bit of garden, on the opposite side of the world. It is sensibility that counts! C.S. Lewis, in our day, directed attention to what he tellingly called '*the steward-ship of the senses.*' Many of us know of his personal awakening to Christian realities, having read his lively, friendly book, *Surprised by Joy.* 'In childhood', he is remembered to have said, 'our senses are unspoiled, though as yet undeveloped.' Expanding this, he added: 'There is wonder in the feel of things – the velvet wing of a moth; smoothness of water; shape of a blackbird's egg; cold strength of a stone; there is joy and life in everything that smells and looks and sounds.'

Some of us, of course, are much better than others at harvesting this life's wonders through the lively use of our senses. Nobody I know of has better laid hold of this than Helen Keller, although limited in so many senses. With what she actually had, she made of life here a glorious thing. I heard her lecture, after her visit to Melbourne and the Braille Library there, and received from her a handwritten letter, thanking me for my readiness to allow some of my books to be made available to the blind in this way. I treasure it: with its bold, square-topped, character-ful letters; as I treasure one of her telling sentences that I already knew: '*Make the most of every sense.*'

Generally, I think of myself as possessing *five* senses; but these days, I am persuaded that that is not all. Science adds wonder to that word addressed to me by my parents and teachers long ago: 'Now use your senses.' The Good News that comes to me is that in addition to the five which I have grown up knowing about, there are at least four extras, known as 'skin senses'. Beyond receiving joy from touch, our brain very quickly senses heat, cold, pain and pressure. And there is known what is now called 'muscle sense' – all the time, with practice, one's brain can clearly know what one's muscles are doing, and can control them. This greatly enlarges the wonder of life here and now. For these I give thanks to God, the Ever-generous, as did Winifred Holtby, when she said: '*I am glad that we have more than one sense through which to perceive the world!*' So am I!

Good News – of Those
Who 'Measure Up'

Two small children were intent on their affairs this
morning, as I crossed from a gate to a barn, to leave a
message for their father. Quite unaware of me, they were
measuring each other's height – a youthfully serious
undertaking of which we all have knowledge. On how
many barndoors, in this world of growing things, have
such marks been scored? My twin sister and I inherited no
certain rules, but we soon made some. It was not allowed
that one should stand on tiptoe; nor fluff up hair over
one's brow. That would have thrown the whole birthday
undertaking out of fairness.

From that early time, I've been interested in measurements. And one of my most lasting memories of a journey
through Palestine with Dr Walker, en route to his hospital
on the rim of the little Lake of Galilee, is a story of
measurements that he told me. The doctor was making a
last round among friends, after nineteen years' service in
the country, so he had many stories to tell.

This one concerned an ambitious young Arab, and I
chuckled over it. Anxious to learn something more of the
big world outside his own hot, sandy spaces, he asked
about the great ships of the sea that he had heard of but
never seen. Dr Walker began to speak of 'The Queen
Mary'.

'But how big is this ship of the sea?' was the young
fellow's first question – natural enough.

Dr Walker replied: 'Eighty-three thousand tons!'

There was a moment's silence – for how could the
young Arab, familiar only with 'ships of the desert',

measure up such a ship? Then, suddenly, he found a way. 'I know,' said he, 'a camel is half-a-ton: so *"The Queen Mary" is a hundred-and-sixty-six thousand camels*!'

Perhaps that was as good an effort as could be expected, perhaps the only worthwhile way by which we humans can measure great things is by lesser things with which we have daily dealings.

A year or so later, I was in Sydney and, leading Morning Worship in one part of the city, I was a guest with others for Sunday lunch in the home of my friend, Lady Stewart. Next to me sat a member of the congregation that morning, Sir James Bisset (to give him his full letters: CBE, RD, RNR, LLD, Commodore of the Cunard Line, Commander of the U.S. Legion of Merit), Captain of 'The Queen Mary'.

As our meal progressed, we had opportunity for talk and I related the young Arab's effort at measuring up his ship.

He laughed! But in a way it is more than a laughing matter. There has always, it seems, been *joy in measurement*, especially in moving amidst familiar things. But there are important conditions to remember, like the avoidance of tiptoes, and the fluffed up front hair; and the carefully worked out multiplication sum, when it comes to measuring a great ship! One poet urges us one by one to consider this, saying:

Measure thy life by loss instead of gain;
Not by the wine drunk, but by the wine poured forth,
For Love's strength standeth in Love's sacrifice.
    Love ever gives —
    Forgives – outlives —
    And ever stands
    With open hands.
    And while it lives,
    It gives.

Good News – of Those Who 'Measure Up'

For this is Love's prerogative —
To give – and give – and give.

(Anon)

One man did this superbly, when the world was young,
moving from the *known* to the *unknown*. His words are
preserved for us in the Book of Psalms (103:2–13, AV):

Bless the Lord, O my soul, and forget not all His bene-
fits
For as the heaven is high above the earth, So great is
His mercy toward them that fear Him.
As far as the east is from the west, so far hath He
removed our transgressions from us.
Like as a father pitieth his children, so the Lord pitieth
them that fear Him.

There is no possibility of measuring God's greatness, His
glory, His love, save in what He has shown us in Christ
His Son, and the New Testament record of His comings
and goings here below.

He did not attempt to explain the inexplicable, or
measure the immeasurable – He told the story of an
earthly father's love for a son who ran away into the far
country. 'That', the Master-Story-teller found Himself
saying, 'is what God is like: that is *the measure of Love*'
(Luke 15:11–24, AV). This, in time, has become our only
way of measuring Love.

The last letter that our friend Marion Riddle sent to us
from India, before cancer cut short her beautiful young
life, was of this measure of reckoning. She began: 'My
most cherished gifts have not come carefully wrapped,'
but she might have said, 'carefully measured'. Our friend
Marion, more than many, had discovered this. She took

31

time to say: 'Our life has had its storm-tossed moments, when gifts of rare quality have been thrown to us out of the turbulent sea of days. One such', she went on, 'was when Anne was burned. I can speak about it now twelve years later. She was two-and-a-half, and it happened in our home at the foot of the mountains in North India. The agony and heartache still bring a nightmare quality. For they are tempered with other memories of gifts of kindness, care and prayers, and in particular, Chetu's gift.

'Chetu passes in the crowd of people who are poor in India, those uncared-for, dirt-begrimed creatures, in grey clothes, tattered and battered by the toughness of living on nothing. His wife is a prostitute, so are his daughters and grand-daughters...

'Chetu had eaten nothing that day when Anne was burned in the evening. He borrowed money in the bazaar and bought two dozen eggs, and came running to our door. The cook separated the whites from the yolks, and placed the whites in a clean basin. (Egg white is an old Indian cure for burns.) Someone placed my hands in the basin of egg-whites. What exquisite relief, and only then did I know that my hands had been severely burned, too!

'Chetu possessed nothing, not even a meal that day. *But he gave more than all he possessed.* He gave two dozen eggs, which were to him more precious than gold and silver.'

> *That God is timeless, my heart knows*:
> Yet I count summer by the rose,
> April by a daffodil,
> And winter by a snow-bound hill.
> And when my heart seems season-bound
> I count love by the daily round
> Of little services designed
> To make life beautiful and kind.

Good News – of Those Who 'Measure Up'

I make *no measurement* to be
A gauge of God's eternity;
And this my heart can understand,
My times are in His timeless hand!

(Anon)

Good News – of New Life

At Christmas I never know what gifts will come to me, but at the turn of the Year it is different. Always there is a neat little package holding a red-covered book, about three inches by four, which never fails to come: it is a pocket diary. And year by year I receive it as eagerly as ever. I use it as an appointment book, to jog my memory of speaking engagements, meetings, visitations, celebrations. Under various dates, there is an italicized reminder of a day's special nature: 'New Year's Day', 'Anniversary Day', and a number of days precious to the Church – 'Good Friday', 'Easter Day', on to 'All Saints' Day' on 1 November, 'Christmas', and back to the turn of the Year.

But my little red book is so small, there are of necessity some omissions. One missing is *The Feast of the Annunciation*', 25 March. In England it is commonly known as 'Lady Day', and celebrates the angel announcement to Mary, the village maiden, that she was to become Mother of the Christ Child.

Dr C.H. Dodd, honoured scholar of our time, attempts to keep our feet on the ground. 'Some religions', he says, 'can be indifferent to historical truth. Christianity cannot. It rests upon the affirmation that a series of events happened, in which God revealed Himself in action, for the salvation of men.' That this happened once, is Good News; but that it continues to be true today, is Further Good News.

We can still visit Mary's little town of Nazareth, as I have done, and stand wordless in wonder on the rim of *The Grotto of the Annunciation*. The work of the village

34

people goes on, much as it must have done in Mary the maiden's day. Her home was not far from the workshop of Joseph the carpenter – no one was far from anyone in Nazareth. The sweet wood shavings curled at his sandalled feet, Mary saw, as she passed on her way to the well, to the market for what they needed, or to the small pasturage to tend the goats. All this was women's work. And she was now a woman, though young. Indoors, she helped with the simple cooking, inbetween times weaving cloth for garments, and making mats.

And then it happened. (Luke the scribe, some time afterwards, setting down her story for matter-of-fact men and women like ourselves, says she was visited by an angel.) Many seemingly enduring things have long since gone – the building which was her family home; almost all of the Byzantine stonework since uncovered in the cellars of neighbouring buildings; and masonry raised by the sweat of the Crusaders.

But the lasting reality has been the miracle Annunciation. Luke tells of it, in his gospel's first chapter (vv. 26–38, AV), as of earth's chief wonder. (I read it through once more, the moment I came back from the Grotto of the Annunciation.) It did not tell me what household concerns Mary was engaged in at the time, the hour of the day, or whether she was alone, although one feels certain she must have been happily employed, and alone, for such high traffickings of the heart. At first, Luke says, she was afraid,

and the angel said unto her, *Fear not, Mary*: for thou hast found favour with God. And, behold, thou shalt conceive in thy womb, and bring forth a son, and shalt call his name JESUS. He shall be great, and shall be called the Son of the Highest; and the Lord God shall give unto him the throne of his father David: and he shall reign over the house of Jacob for ever; *and of his kingdom there shall be no end*.

Then Mary said unto the angel, How shall this be, seeing I know not a man? And the angel answered and said unto her, The Holy Ghost shall come upon thee, and the power of the Highest shall overshadow thee: therefore also that holy thing which shall be born of thee shall be called the Son of God.

And, behold, thy cousin Elisabeth, she hath also conceived a son in her old age: and this is the sixth month with her, who was called barren. For with God nothing shall be impossible. And Mary said, Behold the handmaid of the Lord; *be it unto me according to thy word*. And the angel departed from her.

And Mary arose in those days, and went into the hill country with haste, into a city of Juda; and entered into the house of Zacharias, and saluted Elisabeth (Luke 1:30–40, AV).

This is not a 'Once upon a Time' story, but a 'Once for all Time' story. The Forerunner – Elisabeth's son – was soon born, in the ongoing purpose of God, and then Mary's babe.

How did Luke get this sensitive but wonder-filled story of His entry into this world? Dr J.B. Phillips, a widely respected scholar of our day, in his booklet *Backwards to Christmas*, says:

When the event happened, *by far the most important in the history of this planet*, the facts were known to very few. Did Luke get his story from our Lord's own mother; did he 'interview' the old shepherds on the hills, and hear from their own lips of that strange midnight when Heaven suddenly opened and they were sore afraid? Of course, we do not know for certain; and it may well be that it was not until after the death of

Mary that Luke felt at liberty to disclose the story of her divine conception.

(Told too early, it might have brought Mary under the lashing tongues of local gossips; and that, he would instinctively know, would be unworthy of the miraculous wonder of God's action. As Dr Emil Brunner, one of our century's scholars, was pleased to put it: '*It is the fact of the Incarnation, and not its mode, that matters.*')

'But,' concludes Dr Phillips, to his satisfaction, 'whether it was early or late in the life of the young Church, we may guess that the story was received with joy, but with much surprise. For would not this quiet, humble entry into this world have seemed completely "in character" with the God Whom they already knew? ... In a sense,' he sums up, 'the early Christians looked backwards to Christmas.' And to a miracle, one must add. And I cannot fail to do that, having read so often Luke's gospel; and having come back from hushing my heart at the Grotto of the Annunciation.

God did not take a sudden interest in our world, when first a Star shone over Bethlehem – far from it; He began early to spell out His love for the human race. My dear Dr Russell Maltby (head of the Methodist Deaconess College in Ilkley, Yorkshire) once had a talk with an unbeliever who was beginning to waken to the wonder of the Gospel.

After the doctor had retold as simply as he well knew how, the story of the gift of God's Son, committed to the care of a village woman and her carpenter husband, the man confessed difficulty in believing it, adding, 'But I do know that it is the most beautiful thought that ever entered the mind of man.' 'Then,' asked the doctor eagerly, '*aren't you prepared to believe that God might think that, too?*'

Little Bethlehem, where the miracle of the Annunciation came to its wonderful realization with the Birth, is in some ways today different from what it was when the Infant now widely adored, was born there. I have walked its modest streets, and bowing my head at the doorway that gives entry to the birth site – not only because it is low, but because my heart is full of wonder that I have to do with such a God – Who, 'when the fulness of Time was come, sent forth His Son, made of a woman . . . to redeem' (Galatians 4:4, AV). I have paused before the very spot where once He lay, to take His first breath in our world.

The Jews believed that in the birth of every child there are three partners: the father, the mother, and the Spirit of God. It may well be, although not a required doctrine of the Church, still a beautiful way of stressing the miracle of birth in any family's life.

One of my country's most sensitive Christian poets, Ruth Gilbert, speaks of this unforgettable act of Faith, making one of her life's richest dealings with the same God – a miracle. She has entitled her poem, which she has graciously given me permission to quote, '*Annunciation*'. It begins:

> I have heard nothing –
> Neither voice nor wing
> Informed this winter branch
> Of blossoming.
>
> I saw no vision –
> No tall and twilight guest
> Cleaving the shadow,
> Crying me blest;
>
> No bird of heaven,
> Angel, lark, or dove,
> Confirming all my heart
> Is certain of.

Yet, by the spirit's calm,
The quiet will,
I know and ponder on
The miracle.

Good News – from the Sea

Six minutes from my home is the sea, moving in and out faithfully, of a beautiful bay. The same happens in many other places in our land, and in other lands, sea-girdled.

The same sea, of course, has many moods. Even Sir Francis Chichester had to say: 'Sea sickness is very anti-romantic.' It is! It is all very well to read how the master of 'Gipsy Moth' sailed alone round the world – whilst you sit snugly at home!

It surprises many of us that there is so little in the Old Testament about the sea. Jonah's experience, of course, is recorded there; and the Psalmists register a sense of awe in the sea's presence. They see it, from time to time, overwhelm and destroy life: 'And they that go down to the sea in ships, that do business in great waters, see the works of the Lord, and His wonders in the deep!'

The truth is that the narrow strip of Hebrew home-land fronted onto what we now call the Mediterranean. And it produced fear in their hearts. The people of Bible days regarded it as a barrier, not a helpful highway between one lot of people and another. (Even as late as New Testament times, when John, imprisoned on the Isle of Patmos, wrote of his vision of the New Jerusalem right at the very end of the New Testament, the same idea held its place in their lives. It is recorded in the first verse of the twenty-first chapter of Revelation.) Looking forward – as Dr William Barclay translated for us – they believed that in the great future 'sorrow is to be forgotten; sin is to be vanquished; darkness is to be at an end; the temporariness of time is to turn into the everlastingness of eternity.' '*And there would be no more sea.*' It would no longer divide people from people. And they looked forward to it, as to a dream, that would be realized in God's good time.

The sea is not now accepted in that way, although during its stormy moods, when we cross mighty distances by ship, we have learned to respect it. This was driven home to me during a voyage from Tilbury, London, to Kingston, Jamaica, the wheeling gulls about our portholes all too soon giving way to smashing seas and straining engines. Timbers creaked and whined, and for fourteen days and fourteen nights we were at the sea's mercy. On our second Sunday out, we had two S.O.S. calls from ships in distress. It was an anxious time. I am able to embrace Robert Lynd's words: 'I do not wholeheartedly enjoy storms,' said he, 'but I enjoy having been through storms at sea.' That experience has made me better able to enter more realistically into St Paul's shipwreck, as I turn to the dramatic account of it in Acts 27.

Even to the most daring and experienced traveller, there comes a *last* trip, and this was Paul's last trip. He did not choose it, but was a prisoner being carried to Rome. At first – when he had been handed over to the centurion on board – things went well enough. They called at Sidon, and Paul the prisoner was even allowed to visit friends there – Julius, in whose charge he was, was considerate as well as brave, and he recognized the same qualities in Paul. Aristarchus was another such. The only way that he could accompany his hero, Paul, was to sign on as Paul's slave – and loyalty can go no further.

Soon, aboard a cornship that they had joined at Myra, life was anything but comfortable, as she was forced to take a long way round because of mighty winds. And by this period so much time had elapsed: the Fast of the Jewish Day of Atonement was over in the first half of October, and in navigational practice, sailing after September was hazardous, becoming impossible by November. Like others of the day, they had neither sextant nor compass, and in the darkness of the threatening storm that overtook them, visibility was even more reduced. In their plight Paul, the most experienced man aboard, suggested that they seek some sheltered spot, and stay there till things improved. But those in authority had other ideas. Fair Havens was suggested – but it was a dull little place as far as waiting time for the sailors was concerned. Phoenice was not only a more commodious harbour, but had more of interest going on. But all too soon, a mighty north-east wind struck, and the crew began to throw overboard what gear they could spare. Fear laid hold of all aboard. There was, they knew, all too real a possibility of their grounding on the infamous Syrtus Sands, with a record as evil as the Goodwin Sands to a British seafarer. For cornships then had no rudder, being steered by two paddles from under the stern, and but one mast and one square sail. The fury of the gale put a frightening strain on the vessel – and on its hungry crew. For it was nearly impossible to get food while the storm held. Paul raised his voice, though it must have been hard to hear what he said, and advised them to eat.

On the fourteenth night, they were drifting, and things looked very bad. Then they did something, that those who got to hear of it never forgot: '*They let go four anchors, and longed for daylight*' (Acts 27:29, Moffatt).

*   *   *

And so may we – on land or sea. We have 'anchors of the spirit' which will hold us, whilst we pray.

The first is the certainty of the presence of God – we are not alone. We may be in a strange place; an uncomfortable place; in a foreign land; perhaps in hospital.

Some of the oldtime mapmakers filled in their empty spaces with brief statements such as: 'Here be satyrs and sundry goblins.' When the Spanish adventurers first looked across the mighty St Lawrence, and saw unexplored spaces, they wrote: '*Aca Nada*' – Canada – 'Here be nothing.' But they were wrong: 'Here be nothing?' No! '*Here be God!*' And that is a mighty anchor that we can trust to hold us steady, whilst we pray 'for daylight to come.'

> 'If I ascend up into heaven,' said the Psalmist, 'Thou art there:
> If I make my bed in hell, behold, Thou art there.
> If I take the wings of the morning,
> And dwell in the uttermost parts of the sea;
> Even there shall Thy hand lead me,
> And Thy right hand shall hold me'.

(Psalm 139:8–10, AV)

This certainty is our first anchor, wherever a storm threatens, a crisis occurs.

And the second anchor we have is closely related to it, in purpose and power, to bring us out of the destructive experience. It is *the unquestioned outreach and love of God.* He is there, supporting wholly the cause of right. His Will is on the side of good, not of cruel unconcern. Many of us still manage to think of the Will of God only when disaster descends, or Death occurs. In how many grave-yards have broken hearts engaged a craftsman to chisel on a stone, at the death of a child, perhaps knocked over by a drunken driver or neglected by a frivolous mother: 'Thy Will be done!'

But it is not the Will of God that such little ones should die prematurely – God's Will is good, and wholly on the side of good! An old Brazilian priest, until recently serving in a small village, had the answer for the enquirer about the worthwhileness of the efforts of the United Nations

43

Children's Fund. He pointed to the bell of the church tower, and said simply: 'Once, it used to toll the death of a child two or three times a day. Now it rings only three or four times a month.' And it is the Christian belief that when God's Will is utterly and wholly done in this earth, it will not toll at all.

Let us not forget to let out our anchors – when distress descends, and we pray for the dawn of the new day, needing more than we can do for ourselves.

And we must give attention to the third anchor: the fact that God does not lose even one of us as an individual. This is a needy anchor in this depersonalized age, when many in our midst suffer overwhelming loneliness. We are only grasping the anchor provided when we lay hold of the fact that each one of us counts to God. Our Lord made this very plain, both in His attitude to individuals, and in His teaching. Matthew, sitting at the receipt of custom, hating his job, was yet one called by our Lord. The unnamed woman in the crowd, suffering for years a secret flow of blood that no doctors could stay, was worthy of His healing. A condemned thief, dying beside Him on the Hill of Crosses Three, claimed consideration with His last moments of life. Mary, hastening early to His tomb with her sweet spices, hears herself on that wonderful morning of Resurrection, addressed by her own name.

To hold to this today, however frightening or grief-stricken our situation, is to hold onto a strong anchor. And we are each meant to know it by faith, man or woman on land or sea.

And the fourth anchor in which we can put faith, is the fact that the constructive forces in this world are stronger than the destructive ones! This seems, at times, quite difficult to believe, for the news media lay such emphasis on the startling, the evil.

But in my *Prayers in Later Life*, published by Fount

Paperbacks of the House of Collins, and reprinted in America, I wrote this prayer:

O God, I'm glad that in this world there *are* more good people than bad – more cheerful than morose; more generous than mean. Sometimes, when I read the newspaper, it seems for a moment that it must be the other way round – to the loss of Thy Kingdom, to the discouragement of us all.

Help me to think fairly of what I hear and read, and to get things in perspective. To pass on good news as eagerly as ill news; to give my support to the beautiful, the good, the true. These things (my little prayer finishes) are important to me – because much more important to Thee.

We are not left to face any experience of crisis alone – we can cast out 'four anchors', as we pray for the daylight!

Good News – of a Large Place

It is a happy thing, at times, to look back to the world of childhood. How large the world was then, with early morning shafts of sunlight pure gold! And when the dew, like pearls, had gone from the tall grass, there were games of our eager invention. We hid, and with thumping hearts were found; we outwitted Indians of other tribes; every large tree was as a forest.

And the world stayed large – indeed, grew larger for the fortunate among us, birthday by birthday, as we stumbled upon the world of books. Christian moved to 'a large place', bundle on back, on his way to the Celestial City. So did Mary Slessor, making her way through the dark man's forest in Africa, mixing with strange tribes; so did David Livingstone, doctor, missionary, and valiant heart. And there were books that told us exciting and beautiful adventures in verse – a little harder to understand, but with wonderful stirrings of the imagination, and words that walked on tiptoe up and down in young minds. Strickland Gillian wasn't the only one who tried to put this wonder into words. (His poem was of something I knew about, and now, looking back, can say:)

> I had a mother who read me lays
> Of ancient and gallant and golden days,
> Stories of Marmion and Ivanhoe,
> Which every boy and girl should know.
>
> You may have tangible wealth untold;
> Caskets of jewels and coffers of gold;

But richer than I you can never be—
I had a mother who read to me.

And each of us, in time, came to read for himself or herself. Each birthday, of choice, brought a book; and our little country school set aside a large cupboard for a library, full of treasures. And end-of-year prizegiving brought books with one's name in them: one's very own! I can remember sitting in the grassy shade of the hedgerow, going home, too eager to wait, reading the first chapter or two in each, and looking at the pictures. And with the years – prizegivings, birthdays and Christmases, not to mention explorations of a little bookshop with one's own money – it dawned upon me that there were so many great tales that I would never manage time for them all, or stand with every stout heart 'silent upon a peak in Darien'.

In time, I spent two whole shillings of my own, and bought what looked almost like a grown-up's book (it was that shape), not flat like a picture book for children. It had no pictures – but when I got into it, its words made pictures in my mind. It was called *How to Enjoy the Bible*, and was by Anthony Deane. I'd never heard of anyone *enjoying* the Bible, but in a short time I was doing exactly that myself. It was, I discovered, sprinkled with valiant stories; and the Psalmists wrote songs of joy, as though they too lived in 'a wide world'. One of them, I was happy to find, said as much (Psalm 31:8, Revised Version): '*Thou hast set my feet in a large place!*' Had he too played games in his early childhood, in the long grass? I didn't know. His words may have stood for something else altogether. Perhaps, in those words, he was telling us that he too had entered into the world of music – beginning with simple songs, then on, perhaps, to the excitement of learning to play an instrument. This could be the 'wide place' that his feet had reached. Or it might have been the delight of going journeys in the world, that he was talking about; or of sharing things with gifted friends. (Years later, I read Maurice Baring's witness to such a rich discovery. 'I can't remember,' he found himself writing, 'where it was I first heard Dame Ethel Smythe sing, whether it was in Dover Street, or in her own little house... I remember the songs she sang... and I knew at once that I had opened a window on to a new and marvellous province.')

Music for many of us, as performers, or listeners, is that 'large place' unlike any other in this life: simple things at first, nursery songs leading on to folk songs, to easy hymns, and the great songs of sensitive spirits. And as long as one can remember, there have been the wordless songs of the early morning thrush, the lark up overhead, and the purling stream at the end of the garden, green in the Spring. In time – long, long afterwards – one comes with growing amazement to the 'large place' of Beethoven's symphonies, and the fugues of Bach.

Nor is that all. There is, one discovers, something larger yet: one's growing religious capacity, one's knowledge and experience of God. There is nothing trivial here, unless, sadly, one makes it so. It is a thousand pities ever to believe that religion has only to do with repairing a few secret sins, focusing on a few selfish habits which might be put to rights. It is a 'large' and everlasting place, that makes all the difference to what the days bring. Saint Teresa issued a warning at this point: '*Don't*,' said she, as straightforwardly as she said many things, '*coop your soul in a corner*.' And those of us, blessed with a religious experience that is to us the greatest reality in this world, know that a religion that is narrow and small, lacking service, thought, communion, fellowship, joy and inward strength, may be some kind of religion, but it is not the religion of the Psalmist, and certainly not the religion of the New Testament. Life here – lacking an experience of the Living Christ, matching the needs of body, mind and spirit, with which each of us comes into this world of human beings – can be a very small affair. Sixty, eighty, ninety years of time – what are they? Shining status amongst one's fellows, what is it? I knew I had no need to search further for a telling answer to this, when, on one of my visits to England, I heard Professor Jessop say: 'There's all the difference in the world between seeing life as a meaningful, colourful, hopeful *part of a large life* . . . and seeing it as a losing fight on a lump of heartless earth, where heroism can only be futile and goodness silly.'

Only when one knows that for us each it is part of Eternity, does one know that God has truly set one's feet in 'a large place'. One of the foremost reasons why religion has not gripped many is that it has seemed puny, and lacking in the scope that spells joyous enlargement of life. It has been made to suggest unattractive prohibitions.

Anna Buchan ('O. Douglas') gave us in her family chronicle, *Unforgettable Unforgotten*, a winsome picture of her old father, the Reverend John Buchan. After a full and satisfying life, old age overtook him before he had time to weary. He was compelled to take things more easily, 'but,' added his daughter, 'he continued to make of his restricted life something spacious and serene.'

Exactly!

His feet were set in 'a large place'.

Good News – from the Compassionate

A few minutes by car from home brings me to an open gateway in a wall, backed by a stand of kindly trees. There, set amid shafts of sunlight morning by morning, is a beautiful little chapel. Many motorists hasten by in a stream, without dreaming that there, weekly, a brave bunch of children gravitate for a time of story-telling and singing. None of them comes far, nor easily – they are part of a Home for Crippled Children, some pushed in wheelchairs, others on crutches, or in calipers.

Ministers from the churches in the community take turns in the story-telling; and a kindly teacher of music, from the choir of my church, plays for the singing. (When one of the ministers had to skip his turn, she asked me to fill in with a story. It was an unforgettable morning, and a happy one. Added to the cheerful perseverance of the little ones, was the compassionate background of the Home's staff.)

'Compassion', of course, occurs continually in the New Testament. For instance, in Mark 1:41 (AV) is the account of our Lord's words, and His dealings with a solitary person. It says: 'Jesus, *moved with compassion*, put forth His hand.' The needy one, we are shown, was a leper. And in Luke's gospel is an equally moving story of His dealings with a company of needy ones, all blind, as many to this day are in the East. '*Jesus had compassion on them*,' the gospel tells us, 'and touched their eyes' (Matthew 20:34, AV).

'Compassion' is not a word much on our tongues, these days; but it is still a reality in many parts where the traffic passes by. Dr William Barclay rejoiced to underline the word itself, as 'one of the most wonderful in the Greek language, in which our New Testament came into the world'. It means, in its kindest, most tender sense, 'heart-sorry'. It has been claimed, and rightly, that when Jesus was moved by 'compassion' *He always did something!*

And today, those of us who follow His spirit do all sorts of practical, helpful things. (But some of us don't get that far, we lack the imagination. I stood by, as a friend wheeled a disabled teenager into a youth concert. The Hall's fulltime usher came forward and asked, 'Where would you like to put him?' Not, 'Where would you like to go?' addressed to the teenager himself! As my injured friend commented: 'He is disabled, and in a wheelchair – but he is not wit-less!')

Some of us among the able-bodied do better: we remember that the disabled are still persons, many of them capable of making choices. And we do address them, when a simple matter of choice is concerned such as a seating position in a youth concert. Some build ramps at front entrances, as we have done at my church. Others have other imaginative ways of serving, like the people of Maupin, in the United States, who have added a special troutfishing reserve for anglers in wheelchairs. And what a joy that is proving! A wooden platform has been devised for seven stalls for wheelchairs, each far enough apart to avoid tangling the fishermen's lines. A most practical, and to many ingenious, expression of 'compassion'.

This spirit of 'heart-sorrow' can hardly be realized *without imagination.* A business friend of mine in Glasgow shared a delightful happening in his street the very day before I reached his city. A string of cabbies had suddenly appeared, making their way towards a nearby theatre. He had watched fascinated, and it transpired that a pantomime was shortly to be viewed there, the audience to be made up of invited children. The little ones whom the cabbies carried in their arms, one or two at a time, were from several Homes for the needy. It was a 'compassionate' occasion, a joyous one, the cabbies each with a coloured paper hat. How I should have liked to have seen them with my own eyes.

This same 'compassion' was thoughtfully and dramatically realized at a large Assembly in Nairobi, a while back. An audience from many countries was there gathered, and the person who spoke unforgettably was in a wheelchair. Miss Ruth Elizabeth Knapp had travelled, all the way from New York, to plead the cause of others sharing her world. The vast audience hushed itself, to hear her every word. By no means all, till that moment, had realized the magnitude of the problem.

Some time earlier, for the benefit of the many blessed with good health and natural mobility, the World Health Organization had produced a striking document underlying the need for 'compassion'. 'The estimated disabled,' only a relatively few had taken pains to read, 'is about *four million* – ten per cent of the world's population.' And in an attractively prepared studybook, the World Council of Churches, in Geneva, has extended this enquiry. Aptly, it is called *Partners in Life*. (Seek out a copy if you can.) Earlier efforts had been made by Rehabilitation International. This group was led to believe that, out of the total, about three hundred million were calculated to be *without basic rehabilitation services*. Imagination – as most of us are necessarily equipped with it, to support 'compassion' – is at a loss to understand what this statement means.

Because of that, I welcome E.J. Christoffel's thumbnail sketch of one such needy person. It belongs to their meeting on one of his routine journeys in Turkey, as a missionary to the blind and disabled in the Middle East. He allows us to overhear their talk:

'What is your name, my boy?' I asked him.

'Rasul Oemer oghlu.'

'Are you the Kurdish boy who stays with Mahmud the Kaffeetschi?'

'Yes, Beyim.'

'Where are your parents?'

'Dead. I never knew them.'

'Have you no relatives?'

'No, Beyim.'

'For how long have you been blind?'

'I don't know. I have never seen the light.'

'How do you manage to live?'

'I collect, Beyim' [that means: 'I beg.']

'Do you get enough to be full?'

'No, Beyim, I often go to sleep hungry.'

'What do you do then, my boy?'

'Nothing, Beyim, I just cry.'

'Does the Kaffeetschi not give you anything?'

'Very rarely. He yells and curses when I cry.'

'Where do you put your bed?'

'I have no bed.'

'But how do you sleep?'

'On the floor, Beyim.'

'Don't you freeze?'

'Very much in winter. It's not so bad in summer.'

'Do the people not harm you in town, when you beg?'

'Some people yell and curse when I come. The children often throw stones at me ...'

Says Christoffel movingly: 'Among the masses ... I clearly see his boyish face, so dear and forlorn, and I hear his voice: "*I have never seen the light.*"'

Others of the disabled there are this world round today who are saying, 'I have never run ... never had a full meal ... never worked ... never read.' They are everywhere. Has their grim lot, I find myself wondering as I write this, been better since the United Nations set apart the year 1981 as *The Year of the Disabled*?

I cannot forget the challenge to those of us who are Christian given in the First Epistle of John (3:17, RSV). There is no bypassing it: 'If anyone has the world's goods' – or he might have said: '*If anyone has the world's health, or the world's clarity of brain, or the world's strength of limb*' – 'and sees his brother in need, yet closes his heart against him, how does God's love abide in him?'

It is a challenge!

Good News – of a Green Legacy

All my life long I've had the company of trees, and I wouldn't like to be without them. '*It must be lovely to own a tree,*' said the English home-lover, garden-maker, writer, Esther Meynell, 'I have never done so . . . My tiny cottage garden is too small to take a tree.'

I've never owned a tree, either, even after much experience – from growing up in a tree-blessed part of Nelson; moving, as a student, to the English-like city of Christchurch in the south; on to native forest in the King Country; to a lovely hill in the North, where my friend Rene and I built our first home together, 'West Hills'. Trees were well established there when first we set eyes on that attractive height, with wide-reaching views. Some of them, we sensed at once, would have to come down, if the house we meant to build was to sit there happily in the sun. We went round together, considering each one, and tied a white string on the trunk of each that we wished to keep.

But at no time did either of us flatter herself that she *owned* a tree. Nobody ever really owns a tree. Earth and skies and winds and rains come nearest to doing that.

When 'West Hills', home and garden, knew some sort of orderliness, after many months of hard work, we rejoiced in our trees. Amongst them were a number of young Kauri trees, much prized, thirty feet or more in dignified height. A few months on, outside my glass-panelled study door, I planted another. It was but a stripling, about three feet tall, but in time it would maybe grow into one of our country's giants.

During the sixteen happy years that Rene and I lived at

'West Hills', that tiny tree reached up with its lovely straight trunk – like a child, reaching towards the sky, on tiptoe.

On the gentle blue hills across the valley to the West were others; and far beyond them, out of sight, I knew were many others, blessing a fine Reserve, some of them standing nobly, hundreds of feet high, sixty feet to the first bough. The experts tell us that they stood there *before* William the Conqueror had set his heart on England; before seafarers in their tiny wooden ships had ever heard of New Zealand.

I wondered, as I silently looked out through my study door, would that modest tree – long after I had gone upon my way – be there to bless those who would come? As year by year I watched it grow, I loved that tree. It strengthened my life and vision with a nice sense of perspective, whispering to me the worth of the centuries against the passing moods of moments. Some one might lay upon me a heavy burden; the weather might turn out to be especially trying; the telephone might be exasperating – but always lasting values would there be spelled out.

After sixteen happy years on our hilltop Rene had to seek surgery, and we knew, without words being spoken, that the time was near when we must seek out a level area and make a new home. It was no longer possible to garden to such an extent as we had done, and to come and go from our high-lifted 'West Hills'. (During the last of those rich years, I wrote a book on our home-building, and our sharing with friends who came and went, so that many readers, the world around, knew of it; and when news got out that we were to move a few miles to a level area on the North Shore, a surprising number wrote: 'How can you bear to leave that idyllic spot?')

But we have found happiness in our new home, and its nearness to the seashore, to the library, the church, the bank, and shopping facilities. We have found happiness in our lawns, and shrubs, and attractive pebble garden. It was the right decision, at the right time.

One loss was parting with the young kauri that I had planted – by that time rising strongly towards the skies. *But I did not own that tree*, despite Esther Meynell's words. This was particularly true of a kauri, because it lives so long – up to two thousand years. *It was a legacy to others.*

Those men and women who serve our great forest I mentioned – the Waipoua State Forests – as their contribution to our heritage, know that dealing with developing kauri, they have to reckon on 'centuries between seedlings and stature'. That is a phrase deeply embedded in their hearts: they serve the future. No distance from where they work daily are great columns of mature trees, to let the State Highway through – in appearance, as if through a great cathedral.

There is a saying that has nothing to do with geography: 'Civilization began when a man planted a tree in whose shade he would never sit.' He knows himself part of the ongoing centuries, a legacy that it is in his generous and amazing power to bestow. Someone has put it in a slender poem:

> *He that planteth a tree* is a servant of God,
> He planteth a kindness for many generations,
> And faces that he hath not seen shall bless him.

This can be the glory of the most modest tree-lover, tree-planter. Sir William Beach Thomas loved to tell of a London man who wished, one day, to retire to the country that had won his heart. Midway in his career, he had bought a piece of land and now he wished to carry to completion his tree planting scheme. He found an old countryman to help him. And when next he visited the area where a good start had been made, he found the old countryman full of explanations: 'You did tell me', said he, 'to plant the apple trees here, and the walnut trees there. But it did seem to me that *some day, when you and me was gone*, them walnut trees would shade them apple trees, and stop 'em bearing so well.'

To desire to plant and cherish a young tree is one of the great acts of this earth-life. I am humbled and yet thrilled to think that in a spot I know – and which countless others will come to know, after me – I have planted a tree of beauty, dignity and greatness!

Good News – about Pioneers

Most of our words in common usage have a colour of their own. 'Pioneers' is one of them, a brave, striking word! It came into our language, we are told, from the old French *pion*, a foot-soldier who went boldly ahead of the main ranks of the army to clear away forests and any other obstructions there might be. And in no time, the word was applied to civilians who, in other situations, displayed a like courage. And to this hour there exists no more thrilling word.

I'm not surprised that today Lilian Cox begins one of her prayer-poems: '*Let us praise God for all pioneers, blazing the trail for humanity and for us*':

> For the first man to climb the hill
> And seek a prospect wider still;
> For the first man to brave the sea
> Unscared by its immensity;
>
> For he who, conquering craven fear,
> First found in fire a friend to cheer;
> For he who first from stubborn stone
> Wrought tool and weapon of his own;
>
> For those who first with patient toil
> Did break the clod and till the soil;
> For all such men, since time began,
> We thank the God Who made the man.

And behind each of these, in most instances, was a woman – with gifts of personality, and unique courage, making her contribution. Many a one, a century and more ago, gathered up her skirts, and, with her man, crossed the world in a crazy little sailing-ship, to this land of forests and lakes and waterfalls. We recall these splendid men and women from Britain, Scandinavia, Germany and other areas of Europe. My own forebears were among them.

We live in different days, but we still have our pioneers; we cannot forget them. And today I made a pilgrimage to a fine, short street at the congested business end of the great city where I live, where the whole block, on one side, is occupied by a stately bank building, and the other by a well-wrought Post Office. It bears the name: 'Jean Batten Place'.

She was no early personality, in a tight bodice and a flouncy skirt, as were many of those pioneers whose achievements I honour. She belonged, and indeed, still belongs, to our day. Two years younger than myself, if it comes to that, she was born in New Zealand just a week or so after far-famed Louis Blériot flew the English Channel. Then in 1930 young Jean earned her flying licence at the London Aero Club. (In 1937 I crossed on a new ship, the 'Awatea', from Auckland to Sydney, en route to Britain, and Jean Batten was a passenger, her little plane tied onto the deck.) I have since examined many another such little plane, but only in a museum. Several times I have travelled in modern monsters, and I never do that without a quickening admiration for my slightly-built fellow countrywoman. 'The full significance of Jean Batten's achievements', says J.M. Ramsden, Editor of *Flight International*, 'is almost impossible to grasp today, sitting in a jet, listening to the stereo, and trying not to eat too much. Imagine flying *alone* for almost six days in a wood-and-fabric aeroplane with one engine, no radio navigation aids, and only the most primitive servicing facilities – and all the time just one Gypsy piston beat away from death by shark or wild animal... In addition to capturing five world records, Jean Batten was *the first woman* to make a return solo flight to Australia, *the first* to fly solo to South America and to New Zealand, and *the first* to cross the South Atlantic and the Tasman Seas *alone*. She holds the Britannia Trophy, the Legion of Honour, the Harmon Trophy, the Seagrave Trophy, the F.A.I. Medal, and others. She was given the Freedom of the City of London in 1978.'

And such 'a slight strip of a girl' she looked, from where I stood on the 'Awatea' as the Captain's party proceeded, her radiance and spirit of personality plain.

You and I might feel that it is now too late for such undertakings, as flight has made such enormous progress. But there are endless other challenges. Our world is not yet a peaceful place; nor is it yet a safe place for ordinary men, women and children in everyday affairs. I lay down my newspaper, and turn to read Dr J.S. Whale's words in *Christian Doctrine*, from my shelf. 'Along with the internal combustion engine,' says he, 'there comes the slaughter on the roads; along with aviation, bombs . . . The education which was to have banished crime, only makes crime more efficient, increasing its range. Man's power to do good is always power to do more evil.' That this is no overdrawn statement is a sad and costly fact in our world today. So many living in our midst, it seems, lack those qualities that made our pioneers such courageous and admirable characters. Our universities and high schools have even coined the ugly word 'drop outs', and countless good causes stand stationary, without high dreams, social concern, and care of the aged. And the Church calls us to service beyond discussions, endless seminars, and conferences. One thing we have too easily forgotten: One Person holds the secret in His hands, Jesus Christ. St Peter had to grasp this fact, which many men and women, wanting leadership, fail to understand and to accept gladly. He uses a word which today Dr James Moffatt has translated meaningfully, to draw attention to *One Who goes ahead*, and who could lead us all out of our difficulties. (You'll find it in Acts 3:15, in the Moffatt translation of the New Testament: 'Men of Israel,' says he, 'why are you surprised at this? ... *You killed the Pioneer of Life*. Yet God raised Him from the dead, as we can bear witness.')

And commenting on Peter's words, in his *Daily Study Bible*, Dr William Barclay, after much thought, cannot find a better word than that word 'Pioneer'. For in Jesus, he sees not only the revelation of God's love to us men and women; but the values that build character, and the source of strength that, applied to many of the situations that baffle us in this modern life, would make not a little difference to a few things, but *all the difference to everything*.

Jesus alone is 'the Pioneer of Life'. He knows, and exists within the Will of God. He understands through experience how gloriously satisfying that Will remains, giving supreme purpose to every breath drawn. We ordinary men and women, less perfectly committed, find our heart-hungers tangled with earth values, with material possessions, with cash, with cleverness. Many in our midst lack 'job satisfaction' – to use a new phrase heard today in our labour exchanges, and at the Vocational Guidance counter, and read in our newspapers and journals – because we do not recognize the Pioneer's great conception of *service*. In our expenditure of bodily sweat, and of brain power, our desire is only for monetary gain, and there is no satisfaction there for secret hungers deep in the heart. Only 'the Pioneer of Life' knows how to match those – for never man lived such a wonderful life. (Those who today look back to His days and think Him out-of-date, as did D.H. Lawrence, know nothing of His spirit. Even Sir Bertrand Russell, nearer our own time, looking around on the shambles that man has made of many parts of this world, declared that to come to a new day, 'it was necessary to diminish the instincts that centre around possession'. (It sounded profound enough, and sufficiently up-to-date. But actually 'the Pioneer of Life' propounded that some nineteen hundred years before Russell learned to speak at all, and to try to persuade.)

Another who felt that he was far more up-to-date was Dr William C. Menninger, the distinguished psychiatrist, in the United States. Said he, with surprising confidence: 'If we could love our neighbours as ourselves, we could have Utopia.' (But Jesus said as much long, long ago: 'A new commandment I give unto you, that you love one another.' And again: 'If a man loves not his brother whom he hath seen, how shall he love God Whom He hath not seen?' (John 13:34; 1 John 4:20, AV).)

In short, many of us are not recognizing the Living Truth of 'the Pioneer of Life', much less following Him!

'True Christians', Dr Nathaniel Micklem, with a knowledgeable sharing of this world that we call ours, loved to say, 'are claiming that with the coming of Jesus Christ, there occurred an event as radically new and as incalculably significant for this planet, as when the first living cell appeared upon the earth.'

Indispensable, in this age, is the Presence and Power of the Pioneer of Life!

> *'Tis Jesus, the first and the last,*
> *Whose Spirit shall guide us safe home;*
> *We'll praise Him for all that is past,*
> *And trust Him for all that's to come!'*

> (Joseph Hart)

Good News – at Bedtime

It is a joy from time to time to have an old friend to Sunday dinner. Silvery-haired she is, of bright countenance, a retired teacher, now living alone. But she has such a lively interest in life, she enhances the fellowship of our table.

Lately, she journeyed south to a celebration connected with her College. Many old girls present couldn't help wondering whether, after so long, she would have retained her skill in enabling others to rejoice in good music. Soon, there was no doubt any more. Several who had benefited from this skill fell to talking about it. One of them did more: she set herself to discover the age of the old teacher. It seemed that she was eighty. And, as soon as possible, the recipient of so much joy through music wrote her teacher a little note of gratitude, and with it she slipped into the envelope eighty dollars – one for each year of her life!

Over our dinner-table, our friend kindly gave me her permission to write of it, and I am glad to do that; for Gratitude isn't all that common, these days. Curiously, the word doesn't appear in our Authorized New Testament. Being such a lively Christian quality, I felt sure I would find it there. But I didn't. There is, of course, the oft-told story of the Ten Lepers: all ten cured by our Lord, with only one coming back to Him (Luke 17:11, AV). I had to wait to find the word by turning to Dr William Barclay's gift to me, his modern version, *The New Testament: Gospels and Acts*. It said simply: 'When Jesus was on his way to Jerusalem, he was going through the borderland between Samaria and Galilee. As he was entering a village, ten lepers met him. They kept their distance and shouted: "Jesus, Master, take pity on us!" When he saw them, he said to them: "Go, and show yourselves to the priests." While they were on their way, they were cleansed. *One of them*,' translates Dr Barclay tellingly, 'when he saw that he was cured, turned back praising God, at the top of his voice. He threw himself down at Jesus's feet *in gratitude*.' (There is that lovely word!)

A good time to centre on Gratitude, I find, is when first I get into bed at night. If I don't make a habit of it then, in reflection, in the presence of God, it can easily slip out altogether. But it is easy at this time, when between blankets and sheets. They symbolize for me KNOWN benefactors, to whom I daily owe Gratitude, and the UNKNOWN, of whom the same must be said.

I went, some time ago, to the maritime city of Bristol, a hundred and twenty miles west of London. And there, to my surprise, in St Stephen's Church, in the chantry of a former one on the site, I came on the burial tribute to a Member of Parliament. He had been a woollen weaver in early times, born in 1300, to die in 1380. And night by night, I remember that tribute. It said: 'In 1362, Edmund Blanket, M.P. for Bristol, was the first to set up looms in England after the cloth-weaving revival ... *by tradition, the inventor of an article of bedding which still bears his name.*' Wonderful! (I nearly mis-called him 'Saint Edmund Blanket' – and it wouldn't have been such a bad mistake; many a one has been canonized for less.) He symbolizes for me KNOWN benefactors to whom I owe Gratitude. And the first few minutes when I get into bed, is as good a time as any to reflect on them.

If you are as familiar with your New Testament as I think you to be, you will rejoice that Paul made room in his letters for familiar names of KNOWN benefactors in his life. Sometimes he adds just a postscript, but in Romans 16 (AV) there is a gloriously long list of names, beginning with an outstanding husband and wife. Verse 3 says: 'Greet Priscilla and Aquila' or, as the Moffatt Version says: 'Salute Prisca and Aquila, my fellow workers in Christ Jesus, *who have risked their lives for me.*'

And what had they done, exactly? They were just plain people: Aquila was a craftsman in their city, and Priscilla was a home-maker. We are not told details. She came from a good Roman family. (Dr Adolf von Harnack, a famous German theologian and historian, went so far as to propound the idea that Priscilla was the author of the Letter to The Hebrews, which was formerly credited to St Paul, although it is so no longer.) Certainly it would have been nice to think that in the New Testament was a letter from a woman – but we don't know for sure.

We do have a great fistful of letters from Paul. And the whole of that chapter of Romans is full of names, one after another, headed by Aquila and Priscilla. They kept open house for fellow Christians, members together of what was then an 'underground movement'. For those on the roads, there were then no inns to welcome them; and many were hounded from their homes, threatened with imprisonment or death, because of the Faith they held. It was wonderful for them to come, by some back way, to the door of Priscilla and Aquila, and to know themselves welcome. To exert this homely ministry, these good folk 'risked their lives'.

What the others did, by way of aiding Paul's Christian ministry, he does not tell us, though he calls each by name.

*   *   *

And along with blankets on my bed – going back to good Edmund Blanket – there are sheets. But this is another matter. I have searched through learned encylopaedias and histories, but nowhere have I succeeded in finding any acknowledgement of the originator of sheets – he, or she, is an UNKNOWN benefactor.

So my sheets stand to me, during my reflection at bedtime, for all my UNKNOWNS, to whom I owe gratitude before God. (I've always liked sheets, and when I was still a small country girl, getting into bed between clean, fresh, windblown sheets once a week, I used to tell my Mother that when I grew up, and was rich, I'd have fresh sheets on my bed every night. But that time hasn't come yet.)

Now, I recall that our Master was, long ago, served by many UNKNOWNS, symbolized by my sheets. Early in John's gospel – chapter 4 – is the story of one of them, the woman of Sychar's Well, Mrs Anonymous. Nobody, to this day, knows her name. Only that when she came to the Well in the early morning, or in the cool of evening, nobody spoke with her, they only spoke about her. She was avoided for her reputation; and she soon got to coming in the broiling heat of midday, when nobody was about.

But one midday there was Somebody about – our Master, tired with His journeying, rested on the rim of the Well. He asked her for a drink – and solitary, Samaritan woman that she was, it made no difference, though the Jews and Samaritans were at loggerheads. He gave her back, in wonder and surprise, the greatest talk ever on the meaning of Worship, and the Water of Life. In no time, forgetful meanwhile of the empty calabash she'd brought with her to the Well, she dashed off joyfully into the village, saying to those whom she met: 'Come, see a Man Who told me all things that ever I did: is not this the Christ?' 'Then', says John, 'they went out . . . and came to Him!'

Balancing, in my thoughts, this *unknown woman*, a Samaritan, is an *unknown man*, also a Samaritan. And my reflections are off on the winding, rocky road from Jerusalem high up and down to Jericho (and I've been down that winding road myself too; and it's still hazardous). That day one chanced on a poor fellow, lying beaten and robbed, on the roadside. He was not to know that two men of the Church had already passed by, on the other side, realizing how dangerous it was to stop: the poor fellow's assailants might still be lurking around, bent on their next victim. (And you know the rest of the story, the 'most often repeated story in the world'; and I can read it over and over in the graphic words of Luke 10:25–37, AV. It's a story that lives.)

Some time ago, the French philanthropist, Oberlin, was travelling a like road in Alsace. It was Winter, and he was overcome by cold, staggered and fell. How long he lay there on that rough roadside, nobody knows. It is only known that as he came round, it was to find a waggoner, in a blue blouse, bending over him, urging on him food and wine, and offering to take him to an inn, to safety. At that point Oberlin, bruised, found himself feeling for his wallet. But his benefactor in the blue blouse would not accept his coins. 'Then, at least, tell me your name, that I may pray to God for you,' begged Oberlin. But the only reply he got, with the service, was: 'Only tell me the name of the wayfarer you call "The Good Samaritan", and I will tell you mine.' So he remains to this day one of the world's UNKNOWNS.

We each have dealings of one kind and another, with that man's brothers and sisters. Often I myself don't get a chance to express gratitude on the spot – but I do try to remember such people, as I curl up beneath my sheets at night. People, these are, who point out the way; people who draw to one side, stop, and help me change a tyre; people who will share a bag of plums in a bus, in a year when they're scarce; people, unknown to me, who will bring me good news of their minister's use of my newest book, on a recent Sunday.

Blanket people; Sheets people – the KNOWN and the UNKNOWN. How well they both deserve some real expression of that lovely word GRATITUDE!

Good News – of Good Talk

The day was blue-skied and sunny, the washing blowing on the line! Then the doorbell rang. We weren't expecting visitors, least of all a twelve-year-old lad, his younger sister and their attractive mother. But there they were, having moved house onto a rim of a nearby bay, and this, as it happened, being an unexpected school holiday!

And a very happy visit we had, helped on by home-made cookies, tea and orange-drink as seemed best, and as we were able to provide.

When it was time to part, I handed our House-Book to Andrew, explaining: 'This is where the date goes, this column is for your name, this for your address, and the other one,' I added, 'you can do what you like with.' It is headed 'Remarks', and some people, it seems, choose to leave it as they find it.

But not Andrew, smiling. When they had gone, I picked up the House-Book to return it to its place, naturally looking to see what had been added. And it was young Andrew's remark in the appropriate column that faced me. It said simply: '*So nice to talk to.*'

Continually, and despairingly, we hear in the mass media about differences and divisions; but there is in our midst another reality: communication. Sometimes there are considerable differences in age to be recognized – as in our company this afternoon. But they can be overcome. 'We are dealing here,' as Dr David H.C. Read said, 'with a universal factor in human relationships. Every creative encounter in society involves the mysterious trinity of *thought, expression* and *communication*. We can observe this process in everyday conversation.'

70

(Yet beyond this trinity, there is another: *respect, sincerity* and *imagination*. We must, by these means, get into each other's shoes, for then there is no gap to hurt, between eager youth and grey-haired experience.)

So many, it seems, are sadly aware of gaps – within their homes, their communities, even in their congregations. Some, indeed, faced by this situation, begin 'to talk to themselves'. And this is not 'good talk'. Good talk, my Oxford Dictionary declares, 'is converse, the communication of ideas by spoken words'. Good talk is good, and this was emphasized over the BBC by James Bridie: 'One reason why good talk is good' – as I have just said of our delightful visit – 'is the giving of pleasure to both parties.' It was said of the beloved G.K. Chesterton, that 'he talked into the night, and left behind in it, a glowing track of good things.' Lovely tribute!

All this is true still. Good talk is the most easily welded link between personalities, with experiences, opinions, enthusiasms. Peter and John – with capacities like ourselves, in the early days of the Christian Church – were recorded in the Book of Acts (4:20, AV) as having said: 'We cannot but speak the things which we have seen and heard.' It all adds up to stand among life's most gracious experiences.

(Unhappily, there is amongst us a sprinkling of folk who talk unceasingly, in both private and public, seldom if ever taking time to think. In every bus-stop, in every club, and in every teashop they are – and, I need hardly add, in every class and every congregation. In each place, sweet silence would sometimes be preferred.)

'Good talk is good', especially so where it is most natural, and unselfconscious, although until Andrew wrote his 'remark' in our House-Book, I had not thought to find it expressed by one of his age.

Talk, in this world of ours, has never reached higher than it did long ago on the walk to Emmaus, the little village some distance outside Jerusalem. Dr Luke's account of the famous talk on the road remains one of the loveliest things in our New Testament (Luke 24, AV). One can never read it too often – it holds so much!

Two travellers, heads bowed in grief, turn their backs on the turbulent city. The Young Lord of Life had been arrested in Gethsemane, His tree-shaded place of prayer, marched off between Roman soldiers, falsely judged, and condemned. After a cross has been laid upon His shoulders, a young black man, Simon of Cyrene, visiting the city, and by chance on the rim of the rabble, is brought forward to help Him, as He staggers under its weight. On a hilltop, He is nailed to the same cross and raised high between earth and heaven. On either side of Him writhes a dying robber. At day's end, the rabble has had its fill, and only a few of the Crucified's friends remained, including His mother, Mary. Someone offers to lend his own tomb, wherein no man has ever yet been laid.

But to the two men who now walk and talk together on the road home – when there seems nothing else to do – there comes a third traveller. They never dreamed of a thing like this crucifixion happening – it seems that they have been fooled. '*They talked together* of all the things that had happened ... And it came to pass, that while they communed and reasoned, Jesus Himself drew near and went with them. And their eyes were holden that they should not know Him. He said unto them: "What manner of communications are these that ye have one to another, as ye walk, and are sad?" And one of them whose name was Cleopas, answering said unto Him, "Art thou only a stranger in Jerusalem, and hast not known the things which are come to pass there in these days?" And He said unto them, "What things?" And they said unto Him, "Concerning Jesus of Nazareth, which was a prophet mighty in deed and word before God and all the people: and how the chief priests and our rulers delivered Him to be condemned to death, and have crucified Him. But we trusted it had been He which should have redeemed Israel: and beside all this, today is the third day since these things were done. Yea, and certain women, also of our company made us astonished, which were early at the sepulchre; and when they found not His body, they came saying that they had seen a vision of angels which said that He was alive. And certain of them which were with us went to the sepulchre and found it even as the women had said: but Him they saw not."

'Then He said unto them, "O fools, and slow of heart to believe all that the prophets have spoken: ought not Christ to have suffered these things, and so enter into His glory?"

'And beginning at Moses and all the prophets, He expounded unto them in all the scriptures the things concerning Himself. And they drew nigh unto the village whither they went.'

What Talk that was! No rabbi had ever so interpreted to them those passages from the Old Testament. All too soon, the miles were behind them, and before them the little village, the sun setting slowly, making their three shadows longer than ever in the dust of the roadway. Unable to part with their mysterious Companion, they pressed Him: 'Abide with us for the day is far spent' – and He crossed their modest doorstep, to go in with them.

The travel-stained feet washed, they sat down together to their evening meal with Him at the head, which was a little unusual. And as He raised His hands to pronounce the blessing, there was something about them. What were those marks? They wondered, hardly daring to breathe their questions. Then He took the bread, and brake it in a particular way He had. And they knew! He was no mere traveller interested in two others' troubles; no rabbi wonderfully-learned in the Scriptures; no weary wayfarer · *but their young Lord*! And using Dr Luke's surprising words (v. 31), 'Their eyes were opened, and they knew Him, and He vanished out of their sight.' And they said, one to another, "Did not our hearts burn within us, while He talked with us by the way . . ?"'

The same sun has sought the western sky many times since the close of that talk on the Emmaus Road. But the reality of it comes again to us men and women of faith today, every time we pause to read again Dr Luke's record, or to sing one of our most-loved hymns based on it: 'Abide with me!' Added to these, no prayer that we share in church or home is better matched to our heart's need than Charles Wesley's words:

> *Talk with us, Lord, Thyself reveal*
>   While here o'er earth we rove,
> Speak to our hearts, and let us feel
>   The kindling of Thy love!

Good News – of a Gentle Candle

Off to bed, as a child, in my little white nightie, I never questioned whether it was a candle or a lamp that the Master Story-teller had in mind, when He said to each who followed Him: 'Ye are the light of the world!'

Helping, as I dried the spoons at washing-up time, my small voice blended with my Mother's as we sang what was at that stage my favourite hymn:

> Jesus bids us shine
> With a pure, clear light;
> Like a little *candle*
> Burning in the night.

Going to bed by candle-light was a joy, against the darkness of the vasty night. But there is Further Good News as one grows in birthdays, and in Christian understanding: the challenge of a candle never diminishes. One comes to marvel at the saying 'There is not darkness enough in all the world, to put out the light of one small candle!'

Today, there are many dark places, but the witness of a single candle counts – even in the darkest place. In its most literal sense, a candle is wonderful – there is something in the softness of the light and its simplicity. (Lately, ten thousand candles, desperately needed in earthquake and flood-stricken darkness where power-lines were down, were airlifted to Chile, through the Christian kindness of Church World Service.)

But in its symbolic sense, a candle offers Further Good News, with each Christian fashioned to be spent like a candle! It was the *light* that mattered to the Story-teller – and it is still! A given light. The Master's words that have come down to us are unforgettable: '*I am the Light of the world!* (John 8:12, AV). And immediately He added an encouraging truth: 'He that followeth Me shall not walk in darkness, but shall have the light of life.' And then He went on to couple His prior claim with another, following 'I am the Light of the world', with '*Ye are the light of the world* . . . Let your light so shine before men that they may see your good works, and glorify your Father which is in Heaven' (Matthew 5:14–15, AV).

This is the only thing to do with a candle: set it upon a candlestick, *and let it give itself.*

Dr Jowett spoke tellingly to his fellow Christians when he said: 'Do not let us think we need to be *stars* in order to shine. It was by the ministry of a *candle* that a woman found her lost piece of silver' (Luke 15:8–9, AV). Few of us may have heard of the 'shining' of Natalia Abramovitch, a simple Polish woman of our day. It was only in November 1979 that news of her death was circulated the world round, by the mass media. When I spent time in Israel, moving silently before the memorial there to the six million who died in the days of Hitler's blind rage, I did not know of Natalia. To come to that place of memory, which will be visited by countless others after this, one has to pass through a garden. And at the foot of each tree there is a plaque of a special remembrance, the whole area known as 'The Avenue of the Righteous'. And who are there named? The answer is 'non-Jews who risked their lives to save Jews during the Holocaust'. There, set in silent memory, are names from France, from Belgium, and even from Germany. And added to these, with others, is that of the simple 'candle flame' of whom I am privileged to tell, from Poland.

She was not a great person, a grand person, 'only a modest candle'. In 1942, she was living in the village of

Radonsk, in the south-west, the countrywide situation already grim. Jewish men and women, of every age and personal standing, were being rounded up and sent off in merciless open trucks over the east-bound railway.

At about this time a young man, Michael Steinlauf, came with three others and two small children, seeking a hiding place. Natalia took them in, as there was room in her attic.

But there was a problem: now that she had six to feed, it would be a matter of buying more food, and the authorities would not be slow to notice that. So she set about digging her soil, and planted seeds. But at the end of a whole year, Natalia's guests decided they must separate, and try to find independent hiding places. They were afraid lest the children might cry, and give them away, during a search. Under cover of darkness, they left.

Michael Steinlauf alone stayed, and he alone survived, despite the fact that a few weeks later, there came the inevitable knock on Natalia's door. In the split instant before the intruders crossed her threshold, she somehow managed to give an arranged warning to Michael in the attic. The officers started at once to rummage in her drawers, and to pass from one small room to the next. She gave a pretext of herself rummaging in the drawers, looking for a key – and this allowed Michael time enough to depart.

But despite Natalia's ruse, herself she did not save. She was arrested, put on trial, found guilty of harbouring Jews, and ordered to be shot. However, at that point there was a hitch in her sentence, and she was instead sent from one prison to another. In time she ended up in the notorious Ravensbrück Concentration Camp; and there she remained until the end of the war.

Natalia lived for some time then in a camp for displaced persons near Hamburg; but eventually she got herself away, to live in obscurity and gentle poverty among the refugees in St Louis, in America. Michael Steinlauf had by this time escaped to a new life in Australia.

Hearing of the plan to create 'The Avenue of the Righteous' in Jerusalem, and remembering the gentle soul whose spirit of compassion burned so brightly in the dark setting in which she happened to be, who had saved his life, he asked that her name be set among those memorialized. Later, Natalia was traced by the authorities concerned with this task of Peace and Grateful Remembrance, and thus it became possible for Michael to meet her again, along with a representative of the Israeli Government. And from that time on, the Jews of St Louis took loving care of her. When she grew frail and unable to live alone in the little apartment they provided, they took her into the Jewish Centre for the Aged. And there – white-haired and slow – with dignity and love she came to the end of her days.

Natalia was a simple spirit, with very little education, but the Light of God shone in her heart. A Jewish Rabbi gave the moving eulogy at her funeral, undertaken by the Lutherans, and her name was added to the Garden of Remembrance. (I value her photograph – that of one of the Kingdom's Candles. I am only sorry that when I was in Jerusalem, I did not then know either her name or the story of her shining 'Light'!)

It is Further Good News that in this age Christ has many steady 'candles', where the shadows darken.

Good News – of Good Listeners

Thanks to my travels, I several times saw Dame Sybil Thorndike in the theatre; but only once did we actually speak together and shake hands, and that was on a railway station. She was gracious, she was beautiful, and added to her vital sense of drama was her lovely voice, and a lively sense of fun. But it was something else that marked that moment: *she listened to me!*

Over many years, Dame Sybil – with her husband, Sir Lewis Casson – held a supreme place in the theatre all over the world, and she was again and again the recipient of tributes. But it was an all too rare one in which I am rejoicing, a tribute paid by a dramatic critic, who said of her: *'She was a magnificent listener!'*

Besides any actual physical deficiencies that most of us suffer, there is the lack of concern, the lack of love, of respect, of gentle approachability. But it isn't easy to sum up, since it's a matter of spirit. Many people find themselves willing to give time and attention only to what concerns themselves. Is that, I wonder, why little children are often attracted to old people, snowy-haired, softly-spoken? They make time to listen, and to care about the calamity of poor Teddy – reduced to one button-eye – and matters of like concern. Many of us give only the surface of our minds to this all too rare art of listening. Of one person, all too well known to me, it was said: 'He moved open-mouthed into every relationship' – in other words, he was no listener!

But it has nothing, of course, to do with one's sex. Check it out, and see! In the gracious old parish church in Hitchin, England, I came across an angel on a corbel of stone, instructing a young woman in some important matter. She *appeared* to be listening – but actually only with one ear. At the same time, a young demon was on her back, whispering into the other ear! Too many of us are prepared to give but half of our attention to listening. Only when we offer much more do we receive into our lives certain beauties: a secret truth discovered by a friend; the fluting of a blackbird on a high twig; the gentle patter of rain on leaves; the song of a happy woman playing with her child; a piece of beautiful music rendered sensitively beyond open windows across the street!

Sometimes, it happens that someone with whom one desires conversation, will completely ignore the point of the theme, being wholly absorbed in thinking out *his* or *her* next apt remark. Such is not listening – it is too selfish for that.

Often, it happens that someone will listen for a time – but not to the end. Before that is reached, he or she has broken off into some loosely-associated experience. 'Listening', says William Stringfield, who knows all too well this type, is '*an act of Love, in which a person gives himself to another's word*, making himself accessible and vulnerable to that word.' This can be developed – in the street; at another's fireside; by a hospital bed; within the church hall; across a shop counter; on an otherwise tiring journey. Good listening belongs to being a good person. I have not been able to discover for certain where Dame Sybil learned her secret. I have a much-treasured Memoir written by her son, John Casson, entitled *Lewis and Sybil*, and published by Collins of London. As its frontispiece appears one of the gentlest, most charming photographs I've come upon.

Apart from listening to those close to her, Dame Sybil *knew how to listen in church* – and that is an important secret, too. Especially did she love the reading of the Scriptures, in the noble Authorized Version, which apart from public worship, she read every day privately for her own soul's instruction and joy.

Much earlier, eyebrows were raised, I'm sure, in a Scottish congregation when, with great dignity, Dr Norman Macleod prefaced worship with the Bidding Prayer: 'O Lord, teach us to remember that for every sermon we hear, we must render an account at the Day of Judgement.' It was, perhaps, taking the issue a little too seriously; but I'm sure we could all give considerably more attention to the art of *corporate listening*, as we have the opportunity and privilege of doing in church. It is an important thing to listen there – and to look as if one is listening. For the preacher has done his part in preparation; and in presentation he needs your help, and mine. It's not enough to allow oneself the light luxury of listening as in other public places. One must thoughtfully, reverently, critically receive what comes during worship. The New English Bible underlines this secret, in an account of one of our Master's preaching occasions (Mark 12:37) where it says: 'There was a great crowd, *and they listened eagerly.*' A lethargic congregation can do desperate things to the most able preacher; great preaching has much to do with great listening!

Even though someone is unhappily deaf – as is my closest friend – 'the church', as has been said, 'is a good place in which to listen to God'. And to grow up knowing what life is about, one needs to listen. One has inward needs of a lasting spiritual kind that can't be met until they are ministered to by the Eternal God – in worship, which is preaching, scripture reading, singing, prayer, silent meditation. Listening to God is more than a personal or congregational preference: it is an everlasting experience, an essential to full personality. '*The more faithfully you listen to the voice of God within you,*' said Dag Hammarskjöld, late Secretary-General of the United Nations, revered the world round, '*the better you will hear what is sounding outside.*'

But how are we to do this, being the people we are? We are not always able to get to the known building, conducive to worship, to the loved pew. There are inbetween days of work, travel days, contrary undertakings, desperate obligations. Some orderly session of silent listening is essential! One can get this at rising, maybe; one can slip into an open church en route to college, factory or office; or one can relax on a solitary walk among trees, or along a nearby beach, alone. Or one can sit quietly on the top of a bus, aware of greater things. Any one of these makes a good beginning to the day.

I find myself sometimes saying over this prayer that I inserted in one of my books:

O God, I bless Thee for this wonderful world —
For the freshness of each morning;
For the bright light of midday;
For the sweet calm of evening.

I bless Thee for Thy sustaining presence —
In my high days and holidays;
In times of hard testing and puzzlement;
In times of joy and accomplishment.

As Time goes on, I have confidence —
Since I cannot fall outside Thy care —
In weakness and faltering of body and mind;
Or in aloneness here, when friends cannot be about me.

AMEN.

Good News – of Background People

'Background people' are everywhere. And every meeting with them raises my spirit. Sydney is one great city which has blessed me in this way. Any stranger depending on a traveller's midget pocketmap might well conclude that the distance between Auckland and Sydney is but a hop-a-skip-and-a-jump, they look so close together. Lately, an eager English reader of mine, in a first letter, wrote: 'If I get to Sydney this summer, as I plan, I'll pop over one afternoon, and have a cup of tea with you.' I hastened, before the next air mail left, to uncover our real position. On each side of our blue-green Tasman, there is much to see, with many welcoming cups of tea – but we are thirteen hundred and forty-three air-miles apart!

My first visit to Sydney, away back, was by sea. The city then offered its great new Harbour Bridge, and we sailed under it, gracefully curved against the sky. Next time, I came away remembering its tall new office buildings. And last time, it was its new Opera House, set on its harbour rim, like a bold fleet of sailing vessels smartly approaching!

But I have never forgotten some of its oldest buildings, and chiefly the little Church of St James. Thousands pass it every day without taking any particular notice of it – but nowhere is life possible without its emphasis on 'background people'. Its builder was Francis Greenway, who came from a Bristol family of long-established architects, stone-masons and builders. He was a convict, banished in cruel days, to Botany Bay. The seas that brought him to what is now the fine city of Sydney, were every bit as hazardous as now; and storms battered the 'General

Hewitt', the little wooden sailing ship that brought them, which proved so wretched, that thirty-four of Francis Greenway's fellow convicts died on board.

Yet before he had himself despaired, his feet reached port, and then he began to wonder what he could contribute towards the infant city. Many another – arrested for stealing a loaf for his family, or taking a rabbit from a park, or some such trivial offence, and sent abroad for life – must have wondered what lay ahead.

First, Francis Greenway, with some trepidation, sought out the Governor. 'If Your Excellency,' he dared to request, 'will grant me the power, as an architect, to design and conduct any public work, I will exert myself in every way to do Your Excellency credit...'

And he did! Soon, using his skills, some fine buildings went up under Sydney's sunny skies. The one that remains to please me is the little church of St James, in King Street. It bears a striking tablet, and one that all too few passing notice. It reads:

> In memory of Francis Greenway
> Architect of this Church,
> *And of the Artisans and*
> *Labourers who erected it.*

I rejoice every time I visit Sydney, that somebody set it there, and specially made mention of 'the background people', Francis Greenway and the artisans and labourers who erected it.

St James, whose name that little church bears, was not himself a great leader, or one of the most gifted missionary preachers in the early days of Christianity. Those gifts, with their responsibilities, belonged to Paul and Peter. Like Andrew, and one or two others of 'The Master's Men' – as Dr William Barclay calls them – James was a background man, 'though he was', as the Doctor reminds us, 'the first of the twelve to become a martyr.' The New

Testament says briefly (Acts 12:1–2, AV): 'Now about that time Herod the king stretched forth his hands to vex certain of the Church. And he killed James the brother of John with the sword.' To this day, we know little more about him: only that he was the brother of John, and son of Zebedee. Dr Barclay adds: 'The difficulty in reconstructing a picture of James is that he never at any time in his life appears *apart* from John.' He was a background man.

And all down through the years, the Kingdom of the Lord Christ, Son of God, has been gloriously served by such people – and not least, in the World Church today.

One of the most striking families of our time offers a reminder of the contribution of many, away back to Peter and James. I am thinking of the Niebuhr family, widely known and honoured in the world Church. And I'm not singling out Reinhold, a scholar so gifted that the President of Harvard University, no less, said that he would make Reinhold Niebuhr Professor of any chair of learning in which he chose to serve, he knew so much about so much! Nor am I thinking just now of his distinguished brother, Richard; nor of their learned sister, Hulda – all serving through the world Church. The award offered – in the form of an honorary degree – went, when the time came, to the 'backgrounder' in that brilliant company, their aged mother!

St Paul pays tribute to three such backgrounders in 1 Corinthians 16:17–18 (AV) in very choice words: 'I am glad of the coming of Stephanas and Fortunatus and Achaicus . . . for they have refreshed my spirit and yours.' (They are mentioned but that once in the Letters of Paul in the New Testament – and what a glorious mention: '*for they have refreshed my spirit and yours*'. They weren't leaders, so that their names appeared again and again, they were only 'backgrounders', but what a splendid help was theirs!)

And the contribution of such people is all through the Christian Church to this day, indeed, all through our day-to-day life. I have given myself the pleasure of mentioning again a surprising discovery I made a little way out from Glasgow. I was staying with two cherished sisters, retired teachers, and had my little car with me. 'I won't go into Glasgow today,' I said, early on a day when we were all free to go out together. 'Let's go somewhere out in the country.'

'Let's go to Fenwick,' they said with one voice, 'to Dunselma.' And no suggestion could have been happier. 'You can see Arran from the front garden,' they said.

The day wasn't as fine as that, but we saw much else: we saw a 'co-operation cushion'. And when I've forgotten Arran, and the flower-beds and the fine carpets, I shall remember that cushion.

Mrs Lutterell's room was full of welcome. At ninety-four, she was the oldest of the Dunselma family, spending the eventide of her life in that pleasant place. 'I like to be busy,' said she, 'though I haven't anything on hand at the moment. The cushion is just finished.'

'Mrs Lutterell can't bear to be idle,' interposed a friend. Already I'd been introduced to a second friend on my way up the passage, a little cheery man, Mr Black. 'Ask her to show you the cushion,' he said.

So a message was sent off to Matron to bring it, and patchwork cushion it was, but no ordinary cushion. It was a work of art, its lovely pastel shades faultlessly cut and stitched, for long ago Mrs Lutterell had been a tailoress. And when I went over the fine points of her artistry and praised her she was loth to take it.

'Yes, it's turned out well,' said she, '*but Mr Black threaded all the needles*.' Delightful!

It's no mean thing to be one of Life's background people!

Good News – on Waking

One's first waking moments always matter. The morning comes with its own sweet renewal, for those who sleep well and wake well – although this is not to forget the sleepless and the distraught.

Anne Lindbergh and her young husband, Charles – her splendid flying partner known as 'Lindy', – tell of waking in Stockholm: 'In the morning we were waked by chimes playing "Now thank we all our God" in some distant bell tower.'

Would that you and I could do that, for no spirit better ushers in the day, be it with the sun's first slants, or with raindrops upon the windowpane. During much of his life, Martin Rinkart, the writer of that chiming hymn, had to suffer the ragings of the Thirty Years War – virtually a struggle between Roman Catholics and Protestants. Son of a poor coppersmith in Saxony, he realized, none the less, that with his faith, love of music, and his home, he had *much to be thankful for.*

Eilenburg, the walled town where he lived, served as a refuge for many fleeing from smitten areas, and the result was much overcrowding. Soon, a grievous epidemic broke out amongst the people, and some eight thousand sufferers died – including Pastor Rinkart's young wife. Known amongst his fellows for his compassion, and his readiness to help in grief, again and again he was called to read the funeral service, sometimes for as many as forty or fifty people in a day.

Eventually, the Peace of Westphalia was signed, and the Elector of Saxony not only ordered Thanksgiving Services to be held in every church, but himself selected the text on which each was to be based: '*Now thank ye the God of all, Who everywhere doeth great things . . . May He grant us joyful hearts, and may peace be in our days for ever*' (from Ecclesiasticus). Mindful of this, young Martin Rinkart started a hymn, which in time was to be translated into many languages, until today there are few of us who do not know it:

> *Now thank we all our God,*
> *   With hearts and hands, and voices;*
> *Who wondrous things hath done,*
> *   In Whom His world rejoices;*
> *Who, from our mothers' arms,*
> *   Hath blessed us on our way*
> *With countless gifts of love,*
> *   And still is ours today.*

Where is there a better note, not only in a time of disaster, but to usher in each new day, as Anne and Charles Lindbergh heard it when the chimes wakened them?

You and I cannot often, if ever, hear chimes on waking, but often in congregational worship we are called to join in thanksgiving for our fortunate everyday circumstances, which are far and away more propitious than when Rinkart wrote for his folk. We have peaceful homes, clean linen and blankets, fresh air coming in through open windows to fill our lungs, the fellowship of family and friends, and something worth the doing to get up for. Nor is that all. I tried to write a hymn of Thanksgiving myself one day – but it had its limitations. So I wrote a prayer – and that is within the scope of any one of us who is truly thankful:

O God, Thou art ever bringing light out of darkness, strength out of weariness, new beginnings out of spent energies.

I bring Thee thanks for what I know of Thyself, in the framework of the world ... through friendly human eyes, through books and pictures, through music, laughter and song.

Bless this day all who serve their fellows through their work, through the sharing of skills, the making of gardens, the preparing of meals.

Bless now all too aged and frail to do more than offer their prayers, and their cheerfulness, that others may be helped and sustained.

And may our thankfulness for the fulness of life, be to Your praise and glory. AMEN.

But there is so much more than this brief prayer encompasses. Sigrid Undset, Norwegian novelist and Nobel Prize-winner of our day, moved by her Roman Catholic faith, wrote, in thankfulness to God: 'Let us remember that He has given us the sun and the moon and the stars, the earth with its forests and mountains and oceans – and all that lives and moves upon them. He has given us all green things and everything that blossoms and bears fruit – and all that we quarrel about, and all that we have misused – and to save us from our own foolishness, from all our sins, *He came down to earth and gave us Himself.*'

As small children, we were taught to say a brief Grace at table in thanks for our food; and later, to set this ongoing gift in the framework of the prayer our Master taught His followers to say: 'Give us this day our daily bread.' It was not difficult to learn by degrees that Jesus was not only interested in prayers and hymns, but in bread too. The New Testament stories we read of Him amongst people, teaching them what God is like, showed us that He was interested not only in psalm-singing and solemn faces, but also in food. There was the story of the feeding of the five thousand, heard so early and so often, in church and at home. There was the story of the little daughter of Jairus, twelve years old, whom Jesus raised; and the first thing he said to the adults present was: 'Give her something to eat' (Mark 5:43, RSV). Again, there was that new day at breakfast on the lake shore. Jesus's disciple friends had been out fishing again, after His Crucifixion and Resurrection, and had caught nothing. Tired, hungry, and dispirited, they had returned to shore. The light of the new day had already begun to shine through the lake mists, with a shimmering beauty. The Revised Version of John's gospel puts it beautifully, in chapter 21:4 and 12: '*Just as day was breaking*, Jesus stood on the beach; yet the disciples did not know that it was Jesus . . . Jesus said to them, "*Come, and have breakfast!*" The charcoal fire was burning on the beach, with fish lying on it, and bread' (v. 9).

When the splendour of the rising sun
   First touched the unquiet lake, at morning light
He knew the empty net, the task undone,
   The unavailing labour of the night.
And they were tired: and He, remembering, made
   A little fire, whereon with busy hand
He set His store of fish, and gently laid
   The bread beside it on the dawn-lit sand.
And after Love's strange miracle, they came
   Slowly to land. 'Sit down and eat', He said.
Friend to dear friend, beside the dancing flame,
   He gave the simple fish, and broke the bread.

(Anon)

He from Whom we daily receive our needful food is His generous Father. During many times of the day, we know it – not only in the morning, although certainly then. Life grows complicated, but God's beneficence remains. None of what we call 'our many-tasting food' comes wholly from the giant foodmarket, nor the little corner store, any more than it comes solely from our agricultural skills, our tractors, fertilizers and farmers' seedbags. *Without God's generous aid, we cannot produce a meal anywhere – and still, without us, He will not!*

Beside me once, in a service of Thanksgiving in London, knelt a youth from Holland; beyond him, a teacher from Siam; on my other side was an American girl; beyond her, an Austrian. When we came to the Lord's Prayer, we prayed it each in his or her own language: 'Give us this day our daily bread'. And when we were called to sing, we rose, and sang meaningfully:

> *Now thank we all our God,*
> *With hearts and hands and voices;*
> *Who wondrous things hath done,*
> *In Whom His world rejoices;*
> *Who, from our mothers' arms,*
> *Hath blessed us on our way*
> *With countless gifts of love,*
> *And still is ours today!*

Good News – beyond Waste

One of the delights of tramping is to happen upon a link with a story one has read. It was that way for me with *Lorna Doone*. My memory had, over the years, retained teen age reading. And here I found myself, as a light shower cleared, tramping through that part of southern England where Blackmore set his famous story. Some of our company claimed that the Doones were bloodthirsty characters haunting the wide, wild spaces of Exmoor, over which we were at that moment crossing. Visibility was difficult at times, so that we were glad of the help of one of our number in possession of a compass. He held the less dependable opinion that the Doones were men of high rank, turned out of their estates as part of the troubles of the Civil War. The fourth member of our little company contended that they were associated with a Scottish nobleman who took the name 'Doone' or 'Doune' in an effort to substantiate a claim to Doune Castle in Perthshire. It might have been so, although I was not prepared to argue about it, or it might have been simply that Blackmore appropriated a name he came upon, finding it suitable for the story he wanted to tell.

Late in the morning, with a blistered heel that Exmoor gave me, we all four came down to the little church where, it was claimed, Lorna Doone was married. We, like all who came that way, were shown a window and told about fatal shots fired there.

Hours soon stretched far back to breakfast at our modest Youth Hostel, and we were glad to spy a farmhouse a little farther on, as we turned our backs on the Moor. Our thoughts were busy now with the prospect of a pot of tea, fresh scones, strawberry jam, and Devonshire cream, recalled by one of our little weary company who had been this way before. And indeed, things came to pass, as delightfully as she had foretold.

Half an hour later we left the farmhouse refreshed, to continue down the narrow way of the river, that would take us to Watersmeet. Before we stepped out again, I turned to express thanks to that kindly, capable farmer's wife, and we shook hands. Immediately, I had a query to carry with me for a thoughtful moment – not about the celebrated Doones, but about myself. For no sooner had I reached out my hand, than our hostess exclaimed:

'Your hand is cool! Aren't you warm?'

'Yes, I'm warm,' I replied, 'but my hands are always cool.'

'Ah!' was her response, '*you're a good butter-maker wasted!*'

I knew what she meant, for I had been born on a farm, and my mother had made good, golden butter. Once out of the churn, it needed good, cool handling. But I had never set out to make butter, so I never felt I was 'a good butter-maker wasted.'

I did once have a nightmare, in which I stood before the Lord of Life, in Judgement at the end of my earth life, and He said to me, not as I had hoped He would: 'Well done!', but 'You're a good mother wasted!' But, on waking, I knew it was a nightmare – for I had never set out to be a mother!

But there were persons I *had* set out to be: for instance, a good student; a good servant of the Church; a good speaker in public places; a good writer. I had some idea what had prompted my nightmare, for at the time I was leading a discussion group on the Parables of our Lord, and had been preparing for it till bedtime. We were just about to do the Parable of the Talents (Matthew 25: 14–30, AV) and I had consulted several commentaries, having special concern for the servant who had but one talent and did nothing with it, save bury it away in the earth, as of little worth.

I didn't want to be 'a good servant, wasted.' The idea of a talent is no longer restricted to the use and care of a coin, but holds a much wider meaning. 'A talent,' my Oxford Dictionary delights me by affirming, 'is a special aptitude, faculty, gift – as for music, etc; and for doing – see Matthew 25:14–30; high mental ability, whence talented...' (It is not often that the Dictionary offers a New Testament reference, but there it was.) Here was the sad story of the one man who wasted his opportunity.

Anne Lindbergh, in our day, writes of the ever-present possibility of this. 'I try not to waste any of the day. By waste I don't mean exactly what other people do. *Waste* is being unaware', says she. 'It is spending much time – unaware time – on the newspapers ... on dreaming ... on looking at catalogues; or making too many useless trips up and down stairs; or walking out of doors and not seeing it.'

Another of our day, the great scholar Dr T.R. Glover, found pleasure in pointing out that many of our Lord's Parables *turn on activity*, showing 'how intensely Jesus admired energy and decision, and what a high place He gave to them in His valuation of human qualities.'

But over against this, one needs to consider a complementary truth: it is possible to be over-active, over-busy. Jesus saw that He had occasionally to turn aside, into some quiet place, and He taught His followers to do the same.

For all that I have led a very busy life – and have enjoyed it – I early learned in my typing, picking out letters one by one, that it is possible to be over-busy. There is just one letter different between being 'busy' and being 'bust'.

It is not often easy, of course, in the lives that most of

us live, to step aside from obligations, when the sun shines, or Spring comes, and with simple equipment to turn our backs on routine tasks, in Nature's pleasant green places. But some of us can, if we really give it thought in the presence of our Master, plan some kind of break. That's what we have Sunday for – when ease, silence, and worship count. The old Hebrew word for Sabbath comes from a root-word, which means in this life: '*Stop doing* what you are doing – and do something else!'

My Canadian poet friend, R.H. Grenville, constantly shares with me her sensibility to waste in this good life. Lately, she wrote this, that I hope never to forget:

> Make a space
> in your mind;
> round, like the sun
> (no shadowed corners,
> no rough edges)—
> make it as calm
> as the quiet of leaf-shade
> in a place where the sky
> is wide and patient.
> Then,
> Ask for God's healing light to enter
> and make its own morning.

Good News – about Home

Suddenly, between speaking engagements for my publishers in London, I found myself free to go to the Ideal Home Exhibition. I had heard much about it, and read magazine and newspaper advertisements. As the old lady said, buying herself a new electric eggbeater: 'They spoke of it very heartily in the advertisements.'

I had no idea of the size of the Exhibition, nor how it would be set out; but I was impressed. Only my twelve thousand miles distance from home saved me from real temptation – that was too far to convey purchases. I could have bought a new carpet and many more items: a lately-designed iron, though I had a reliable old friend at home; a modern whistling-kettle, when I could lift my own kettle the moment it boiled; an electric sewing-machine that promised miracles, but I did very little sewing that our old hand-machine couldn't deal with. And there were super-easy-chairs, the like of which my mother, who had been by far the best home-maker I had closely known, had never owned in all her life. She had contented herself with a newly-covered cushion, or a length of flowery cretonne from the furnisher's roll, to restore her old chair, and both were attractive, and serviceable for years.

In our farm-home, like every other around us, were oil lamps, and kindly candles. Few things changed until an overwhelming flood carried away all our topsoil. Then our beloved farm paddocks stood bare, our stacks had blown down, and our house-cow was carried off in the swirling waters to spend days and nights down the river, washed up on an up-ended willow tree.

We moved a few miles to an old house in the village,

two-storeyed and the first thereabouts to have electricity – thanks to a miracle-making man up at the flour-mill. People came to see what we had, and we young folk took our first timid steps into this 'button-pressing age' in which we would grow up. The fact that we had then no running water indoors added up to no inconvenience – we had an old pump at the back door, from which beautiful sparkling water issued, and we drank it with joy, or carried it indoors in a shiny kettle to the black, wood-burning iron stove. On Monday mornings early, faithfully, week by week, we boiled up the old copper where it stood, and by breakfast-time, beyond our green cow paddock, our washing billowed on the line – spotless sheets like the Armada coming up the Channel.

It was a welcoming home – friends, in ones and twos, liked to visit, especially those who knew our parents' gift for breadmaking, buttermaking, fruit preserving, and gardening. They always went back home with baskets bulging in Summertime, when the orchard was plentiful, and the garden too in its own way.

When we wanted music beyond what the blackbird and thrush could supply, we had our tall piano in the front room, and over in a corner our Edison phonograph, with an immense horn like a metal convolvulus, and wax cylinders. On winter evenings, neighbours came to marvel at these, too. Our parents were secretly marked out as 'most adventurous'.

When I came home for the summer vacation, as a young adult student from Christchurch, in the south, a little red single-seater Singer car was parked in the disused trap-shed. So came into our lives another wonder, and I took my first car ride, sitting in its luggage space behind a neatly folded canvas hood, exposing a rider to the elements. My twin sister and young brother were still at home, but they couldn't be expected to think, as I did, about the goodness of our home. I had been away. And I had somewhere

happened upon a quotation from a poet scarcely known
to me then, George MacDonald. 'Father and Mother', he
said, 'are Home, not the house we were born in.' I copied
it out, though I hardly needed to. And years on, I
approached all the gracious furnishings and helpful and
cunning gadgets in the Ideal Home Exhibition, in terms of
it.

In time, I sent out into the world the first of my books,
and there quoted – with kindly permission – something
that my first editor, Dr Leslie Church, wrote: 'It is
people,' he said, 'close-linked in unselfish relationship,
who make homes; and it is the spiritual relationship of man
to his Maker which gives him Home as the goal of all his
pilgrimage.'

Week by week, in those home days, we went to worship
in the little chapel on the corner opposite. There I had
embraced many Christian values, to which I now added
these underlined by Leslie Church. 'One cannot', he
added, 'learn the secret of an ideal home, from a primer
on architecture, or a journal on house furnishing.'

Some years on, one gentle evening, our mother suddenly died in that loved house; and a few years later, when
our father was on a visit to relations afar, it burned down.
(A swarm of bees had settled in its front room chimney,
and the woman who at that time occupied the house, made
a little fire of chips and brown paper, to smoke them out
– and somehow, she overdid it. Unknown to any of us,
there may have been a crack in the chimney.)

Much later, a new one-storeyed house was raised on the
site – but it was never the same to any one of us. Today,
on the five-acre garden where our home stood, a number
of new houses now stand, approached by 'Snowden
Place'.

An 'ideal home', of course, can be builded anywhere,
if love and respect are present and people know belonging,
and fit in without grousing. Home is the place where big

dreams are shared, and small things count – where good laughter is more important than an electric button to press. The young will go far towards picking up lasting values – from unspoken attitudes; from talk around the meal table; from how the front door is answered when a knock is heard; and from what is said after the caller is gone.

To such people, religion is not just a matter of going to church, but of what one comes to know of the inwardness of worship and service, and of loving loyalties. Each in the home has his or her body, mind and spirit – with corresponding needs. Some are fortunate to receive a little religious teaching at school, but much depends on whether or not the teacher has a real faith. Lord Bryce, when asked what he thought would be the effect of the absence of such teachers from schools, replied: 'I can't answer that – *not till three generations have gone by.*'

That is a test. Often a *first* generation holds closely to religion; a *second* attends worship on special occasions; a *third*, only when involved in family or business weddings, funerals, baptisms, or some community or national celebration.

And life is much more. Religion is of small account unless it is woven of every part of home's relationships, choices, joys and sorrows. Third-generation Christians know all too little, or often nothing, of the supremacy of Christ, the valiancy of the faith in places of business, of suffering, and of adventurous enterprises for common good in the world.

Many 'average people' loosely do just what they feel like – work on a day, leisure day, Sunday – and wonder why life doesn't add up. Such should lend an ear to detective-writer Dorothy L. Sayers, a thoughtful modern Christian. Asked to address a letter to average people of the third generation, she replied plainly: 'The only letter I ever want to address to "average people" is one that says: "Why, when you bestir yourselves to mug-up terms about electricity, won't you do as much for theology, before you begin to argue about it? I do resent your being so ignorant, lazy and unintelligent. *Why don't you take the trouble to find out what is Christianity, and what isn't?*'"

This is a task that starts early – and at home!

Good News – of Words and Deeds

Over a long time I've learnt some lasting things from children, in classes, clubs, and libraries. I think of little Olive Schreiner, whose parents married in London, and moved out to Africa in a crazy little sailing ship. Cape Town interested them to start with, but then they moved eastward, to live in a little daub-and-wattle house.

Soon, as missionaries, they were on their way again, this time in a great ox wagon, with loud, crunching wooden wheels. Always Father sat up in front, with a firm hold on the reins, and holding a fine whip, its lash of hippopotamus hide ending in a stinging strip of antelope skin. One evening about sunset, having covered many miles, with their bundles and pots and pans they came to a halt. There, in a barren place, they settled, and under a thatch of straw they made a new home. When velvety darkness descended, it was a bit creepy: often, dwarf bushmen danced around the house, with lions roaring at a distance, and jackals and hyenas prowling. But the little family got used to it.

With each new arrival, a new room was added. The days were full of crowded activities, and always at night there were stories to share. Mother and Father had many adventures of their own that the children loved to hear again and again – and always there were books. They felt themselves a close, happy little company, set in the great spaces. In time, little Olive came to the age where she could read for herself, and happily discovered, one after another, some of the most wonderful stories in the world, nestled within the New Testament.

There came a day when her mother, having an infrequent visitor, was busy serving tea, and sharing news. Little Olive was among her books, in another room, and time passed happily. But after a pause, she rushed into the room where her mother was serving her visitor. 'Oh, Mummy,' she exclaimed, pointing to her New Testament, *'look what I've found! Isn't it lovely? Now we can all live like this!'*

Her mother and her friend smiled – but it was right. For the stories of Jesus, transcribed into the New Testament, weren't just to read in a solitary hour, but were to translate into action. The Master-storyteller had made that plain. Said He: 'If ye know these things, happy are ye if ye *do* them' (John 13:17, AV).

Words pull us up at times in our journeying, many of them with striking colour and meaning, but alone they have never been enough. I couldn't have been less excited than little Olive when this dawned on me, and later, I saw it beautifully stated in the New Testament (1 John 3:18, Moffatt Version): 'Let us put our love *not into words or into talk, but into deeds, and make it real.*' And from hour to hour, down the long years of life's challenge, this has remained true. Little Olive had emphasized the right measure of involvement: hers were clear, adventurous words. She did not know that a learned, world-famous man (Professor Harnack) had put it like this: 'The theologians of every country only half discharge their duties if they think it enough to treat of the Gospel *in the recondite language of learning, and bury it in scholarly folios.*'

Little Olive used more attractive words, and more active ones. Her Christian emphasis was right – part of the ongoing Gospel of our Lord! Words have colour and meaning and delight – and words are essential.

Religion's all or nothing; it's no mere smile
O' contentment, sigh of aspiration, sir —

No quality of the finelier-tempered clay
Like its whiteness or its lightness; *rather stuff
O' the very stuff, life of life, and self of self.*

(Browning)

People about us are not satisfied just to *hear* Christianity
in words, for all that we do occasionally, in church, hear
it beautifully spoken. They want to see it in life, in action,
in deeds. Old John Lydgate, away back in 1400, put it well
when he said: 'Woord is but wynd; *leave woord and take
the deede.*' And after many centuries of speaking,
teaching and living, nothing has happened to alter this
emphasis. 'In our era,' said the leader of the United
Nations, as earnestly as he knew how, 'the road to
holiness necessarily passes through the world of action.'
Everything, these days, is coming under judgement:
Christian worship, church conferences, meetings for
fellowship, witness of any kind. At some of these we find
ourselves facing an Agenda. I have faced many, but have
never, until now, looked up the exact meaning of this
commonplace word in my dictionary. It is not something
to be talked about – it is '*something to be done*'. A fellow
committee member once passed a scrap of paper along the
board table to me – being another person at the mercy of
a dull, lengthy speech – and on it he had written: 'Words,
Words, Words!'

Our Master used words beautifully, tellingly. Some
very experienced listeners once said of Him: '*No man
ever spoke like this man*' (John 7:46, RSV). But it was His
deeds that have stayed longest in men's minds! And of
those who have followed Him through the centuries till
today, the same can be said. Sir William Osler, the great
scholar and physician of our era (he died in 1919), held his
first chair of medicine at McGill University; he became
professor of clinical medicine at the University of

Pennsylvania; and then, at the age of forty, accepted the chair of medicine at the famous Johns Hopkins University. Soon he was appointed a lecturer at the Royal College of Physicians in London; and at fifty-six he became regius professor of medicine at Oxford. A versatile man! He moved about a great deal, and wrote what has been counted 'the most popular textbook in the English language with several generations of medical students and practitioners'.

But for all that Osler was a profoundly learned man, commanding many words, *he added to the enrichment of life*, far more than the mere words of his lecture rooms and textbooks. It spilled over into the lives of those who knew him first in hospital – patients, doctors and nurses. One person tells of Osler's interest in ordinary people, and how he met him walking down a main street one bitter night in Montreal. Seeing the man without a coat, Osler took his own topcoat off his own back. And his biographer took leave to add: 'It is singular how all who were thrown with Dr Osler *felt his likeness to Christ.*'

The doctor was not a man of words only – far from it. His secret, which is our Master's secret, has been in words for many years, awaiting our acceptance in our day-to-day life:

> *To do Thy will* is more than praise,
> *As words are less than deeds*;
> And simple trust can find Thy ways
> We miss with chant of creeds.

(Anon)

Good News – about Surprises

Rene and I have hastened into the lounge three times in the last hour!

Early, the front doorbell rang, and when I answered it there, to our pleasure, stood an artist friend from eighty-odd miles away, a neatly-wrapped package under her arm.

When she was indoors and seated, we learned that Mary's package was for us – one of her own exhibition prints, already attractively framed, a bluey-green, delicate thing, *Floating Feathers*.

After she had taken leave of us we set to finding a suitable place to hang it on the remaining wall space of our flat. It gave us pleasure to do that, for those little fluffy feathers were now in our lives, as we returned to our jobs.

Presently, I found myself recalling J.M. Barrie's sharing of a family situation. In their simple days of home-making, they acquired a new set of chairs, the like of which they had never had, and every now and again, in that early joy of possession, they ceased what was on hand and, opening the parlour door, burst in, '*to take them by surprise!*' And it's a good secret!

We had never before had an artist's original print on our walls, and three times within the hour, it seemed only fitting to dash in 'and take it by surprise!'

I will not lightly use that common phrase, and speak of it as 'The surprise of our lives' – we have shared a good many surprises by now – but it certainly added something to our lives that was not there before.

The God Whom we adore, and serve in our daily lives,

is a God of surprises, because He is a God of Love. A contemporary novelist has led us joyously towards this reality, in saying: '*There is no surprise more magical than the surprise of being loved*; it is the touch of God's finger on man's shoulder.' It is! And to trudge through days and years of this earthly life without coming upon this great reality, is a grievous loss.

Dr George Morrison underlined this discovery, and wrote for us: 'Expect surprises! Have an open eye. Believe that there are more things in heaven and earth than have been dreamed of in your philosophies. And then, when common actions are irradiated, and common lives flash into moral glories, when the mysteries of life, and love, and death so baffle us that we can only say with Paul, "We know in part" – we shall be nearer ... than we dreamed.'

To count on the fingers of one's hands the surprises clearly recorded in the New Testament, without even turning back as far as the Old, is a good thing to do. One can't do it too often! Away back in time – Elisabeth, wife of Zacharias and mother-to-be of Christ's forerunner John the Baptist, was blessed with what was literally 'the surprise of her life'; and Zacharias likewise (Luke 1:11–14, AV). At first, it issued in fear; but soon both were reassured, and grateful wonder took the place of fear. 'Fear not, Zacharias,' were the words of God's angel visitant, 'your wife Elisabeth will bear a son to you, and you must call his name John.'

But none, in the purposes of God, could have been more surprised at any such happening than the village maiden, Mary, who was betrothed to the carpenter, Joseph, belonging to the house of David. (A little while back, I trod the hill-surrounded streets of Ain Karim, Elisabeth's quiet village, outside Jerusalem, and later, the little dusty streets Mary and Joseph knew, in the village of Nazareth. It was easy then, to recall these people blessed by God's surprises – and every Christmas brings back with striking actuality this expression of the Love of God.)

Out on the very Shepherds Fields that one can see today, near the birthplace, down-to-earth working men tended their sheep by night, under a starry sky John Erskine chose his words well, imagining, in modern mood, how it must have been for at least some of that little company, who were also at first filled with fear:

> Out of the midnight sky a great dawn broke,
> And a voice, singing, flooded us with song.
> In David's city was He born, it sang,
> A Saviour Christ the Lord. Then while I sat
> Shivering with the thrill of that great cry,
> A mighty choir, a thousandfold more sweet
> Suddenly sang, Glory to God, and Peace —
> Peace on the earth; my heart almost unnerved
> By the swift loveliness, would hardly beat.
> Speechless we waited, till the accustomed night
> Gave us no promise more of *sweet surprise*;
> Then scrambling to our feet, without a word
> We started through the fields to find the Child.

(Anon)

God's next 'surprise of Love' was that this same Son should be chosen to grow up in the little, often-despised, village of Nazareth, in a carpenter's home and workshop rather than in the home of one giving his whole life to religion. God's Son, very surprisingly, had His place at a workman's bench, surrounded often by woodshavings. To Him, the farmers brought their broken plough-beams; the wives, their wooden chests; the children, their damaged toys to be given back into eager hands. When He, whilst yet young, latched the shutters of His workshop, and started preaching, teaching and healing, *the people were surprised* – and no wonder! (Luke 4:22, AV). 'All bare Him witness, and wondered at the gracious words which proceeded out of His mouth. And they said, Is not this Joseph's son?' To some it might have seemed a striking thing that He began His ministry in the little familiar town, where His customers lived – and yet, how fitting it was! There was nobody in the company gathered who could say: 'I did business with You – but it was a shoddy deal.' No one! No father of a family could say: 'I ordered a stool to be made, and when we used it, we found it never stood level and dependable.' No young housewife in that company of listeners could say: 'Mr Carpenter, you recall that chest for my things, before I married? I have to say that the lid never fitted, and the moths got in!' The young carpenter, turned preacher, teacher and healer, knew well what He was doing when He began His ministry in Nazareth, where everybody knew Him. Not a soul could raise a contrary voice. His plough-beams fitted smoothly, no beast was ever galled by rough workmanship from Him; no child ever went crying to bed, because his toy wasn't properly mended. His integrity was confirmed by a voice out of Heaven, that many of them heard when He went down to Jordan's bank with others for His baptism. As He came up out of the waters, 'lo a voice from heaven, saying, *This is My beloved Son, in Whom I am well pleased*' (Matthew 3:17, AV).

But what had He done, by then, that so pleased God? He had not preached a single sermon; not told a striking parable that would echo through the years; nor had He restored a single sick body to health. No! But He had done a good carpentering job – and that was what He had been called to do, at that stage!

For all its surprising rightness, this service of Life, and later of Death, lasted beyond political schemers, religious zealots, soldiers, and the common rabble of the city of Jerusalem, bludgeoning Him, setting a cross upon His back, and ridiculing Him, even whilst He hung between two robbers to die.

But that was not all – God's surprises were not at an end! Though He died, and was buried in a borrowed tomb, there was a third day. In a short time, two downhearted followers were on their way home, heads down, discussing their grief as they went. And they were joined by another, who asked what their trouble was. They responded with the understandable assumption that He must be only 'a stranger in Jerusalem', and unaware of the dastardly deeds of the previous few days. And when He asked them 'What things?' they went through all the shame and despair they had experienced, that made up the grim happening of the Crucifixion... '*Though some women of our company*'. (as Dr James Moffatt reports it in Luke 24:22), '*gave us a surprise!*' And what surprise was that? 'They were at the tomb early in the morning, and could not find His body...!'

Alas, there are some amongst us today – despite the witness of countless wayfarers who have met the Living Christ on their way through this life – who are at a loss to accept God's Surprise of the Resurrection! And it shows in many ways. Dr William Robertson Nicol said that he expected Christians, when gathered together, 'to be men and women who would show Surprise above all things'. But it wasn't often so. What struck him, he had to confess, 'even in many present-day worship services, was *the absence of the element of Surprise* – surprise of diction, surprise in thought!'

And there still remain among us Christians who have not caught up with the great modern-day Roman Catholic leader, Cardinal Suenens, who said at Pentecost in 1974: '*I believe in the Surprises of the Holy Spirit.*'

Nor is that the end of what Christians can count on. There is Further Good News. The twenty-fifth chapter of Matthew's gospel offers us a word picture as dramatic as any in the New Testament. It is full of surprises! The only response the commendation of the King of Glory brought forth from some who had done kindly actions, and which they had forgotten, was: 'When saw we Thee a stranger, and took Thee in? or naked, and clothed Thee? Or when saw we Thee sick, or in prison, and came unto Thee? And the King shall answer and say unto them, Verily I say unto you, Inasmuch as ye have done it unto one of the least of these My brethren, ye have done it unto Me!' (And a tragic Surprise awaited those who had done what they counted as worthy – but which was lacking the Spirit of Christ: they went away into 'Outer Darkness!')

Fullness of Life after Death – for those redeemed by Christ – is the great climax of Christ's Judgement. Dr William Temple, a beloved Archbishop of Canterbury in our century, loved to say: 'There is nothing in the world of which I feel so certain. I have no idea what it will be like, and I am glad that I have not. I do not want it as mere continuance, but I want it for my understanding of life!'

It is a loss beyond imagination to let the 'Oh's!' and exclamations of Joyous Surprise fall from our Faith!

> *I know not what the future hath*
> *Of marvel or surprise,*
> *Assured alone that Life and Death*
> *His mercy underlies!*

Good News – from Silent Stones

Five or six times in a morning, as I lift my eyes towards my large study windows, I see the sturdy tower of the church where I worship. It is not an old church, as was the first one I knew, the parish church where I was christened in the village. That nestled between great trees, amid the stones of those we children later called 'the sleeping people'.

There, I suppose, began my interest in epitaphs, and it was quickened when in my twenties I journeyed to the old world, and first stepped into England. From my first day in London, I began reverently to seek out epitaphs, beginning with that of Susanna Wesley, the beloved and honoured mother of John and Charles, and the remainder of that large family. It was easy to find, for Bunhill Fields, which provided her last resting place, was right opposite Wesley's Chapel and House in City Road, together with the Epworth Press, my first publishers.

Susanna, I learned, was buried on Sunday the first day of August, 1742. John read the funeral service of the Church of England, and Emilia, Susanna, Hetty, Anne and Martha stood round with a great company of friends assembled. A hymn was sung, and John preached one of his most impassioned sermons. Later, a plain stone was set up, with an epitaph in verse, penned by Charles. (The original stone having suffered from age and weather, a new stone, with a fresh inscription, was set up in 1828.)

Further Good News

Here lies the body of
MRS SUSANNA WESLEY,
Widow of the Rev. Samuel Wesley, M.A.,
(Late Rector of Epworth, in Lincolnshire)
who died 23rd July, 1742,
Aged 73 years.
She was the youngest daughter of the
REV. SAMUEL ANNESLEY, D.D., ejected by the Act
of Uniformity from the Rectory of St. Giles,
Cripplegate, August 24th, 1662.
She was the mother of nineteen children,
of whom the most eminent were the
REVS. JOHN AND CHARLES WESLEY;
the former of whom was, under God, the
Founder of the Societies of the People
called Methodists.

In sure and certain hope to rise,
And claim her mansion in the skies,
A Christian here her flesh laid down,
The cross exchanging for a crown.

Long and inclusive – as were many epitaphs of the day –
it is dignified. All too many could scarcely make such a
claim. Within a few paces of Susanna's gravestone is
another, almost incredible in these days. It reads (and it
took me some time to copy its words): 'Here lyes Dame
Mary Page, relict of Sir Gregory Page, Bart: who departed
this life on the 11th day of March, 1728, in the 58th year
of her age.' She died, I could only assume, from dropsy,
poor dear; for her epitaph went on to say: 'In 67 months
she was tapped 66 times and had taken away from her 240
gallons of water, without ever repining at her case or ever
fearing the operation.' What courage!
All over England, the workmanship of local poets –

many of whom earned their 'baccy money' this way – are to be discovered still. And, as the old saying runs, '*where moss has grown, grief has departed*'. The most interesting ones came in the early seventeenth century. Added to the limitations of village verse was often a certain eccentricity, even whimsicality. Typically, the Wesleys had nothing to do with this approach to Death, showing instead a simple, sorrowing dignity, with a confident faith in the life hereafter. Few of their 'sleeping places', as we children called them, even had epitaphs. (And when the Wesleyans migrated in sailing-ships to my own country, the same was true.) I was the more surprised, for this reason, to find a cemetery around a little Methodist church, an hour's run to the north, which I had to visit in the course of my ministry. I had pulled into the small farming community, with my car and caravan, thinking to park down on the flat by the houses. But when I approached, I learned from a kindly man of the church, who met me, that the low-lying community was flooded. He asked me whether I 'would mind sleeping the three nights in the cemetery' – on the hill, where he met me – 'I have mowed the grass there for you,' said he, 'so that you won't get your feet wet.' I thanked him; and set about establishing my caravan.

And I had three good sleeps in that cemetery – the only time in my life that I've done such a thing. Whilst there, I copied out the wording on some of the old stones, but there was nothing memorable, much less eccentric. One needs to forage in the old graveyards of England for that, grass-grown, many of them, moss-covered, guarded by great trees.

Some of their versifiers, it seemed, aimed at topicality above all. In Moreton-in-Marsh, my guidebook told me, was an old epitaph recording a personal tragedy. 'The site of a Norman church', my book said, 'has been found in the Congregational cemetery, and the new church, which consists mainly of nineteenth-century work, has little of interest except perhaps the efforts of an old rhymester:

> Here lies the bones of Richard Lawton
> Whose death, alas, was strangely brought on;
> Trying one day his corns to mow off,
> The razor slipped and cut his toe off.

I could not find Richard's stone, though I sought patiently for it, and told myself that it had likely become mossed over. The day was drawing to a close, so I knocked at a nearby cottage, seeking help. But the shy body who opened the door to me, didn't know of it. Then she added: 'I've lived here a long time. And I'm fond of my church, but I don't know nothing about the dead – only the living.' And with that, and the closing of day, I had to give up my search.

A month or so later, I sought one of Cheltenham's most famous epitaphs. My feet had led me that way, on an itinerary designed by my publishers. It was pleasant seeking in the well-kept graveyard of the parish church. I found John Higgs', the pigkiller's, stone, with his life's occupation somewhat clumsily worked in.

The blacksmith, John Paine, who died August 30th, 1786, aged 72, got much the same treatment. One can imagine a good, well-filled pipe, enjoyed by some local, for supplying words that John Paine, in life, might not have had the skill to provide:

> My sledge and hammer lies declined,
> My bellows pipe have lost its Wind,
> My Forge is extinct,
> My Fire's decayed,
> And in the dust my Vice is laid,
> My Coal is spent, my Iron's gone,
> My Nails are drove, my Work is done.

But the most famous epitaph Cheltenham boasted, I could not find; nor could my kind hostess. Perhaps weather and time had removed the unbelievable lines:

> Here lies I and my two daughters,
> All along drinking Cheltenham waters.
> If only we'd stuck to Epsom salts
> We wouldn't be lying in these here vaults.

*　*　*

But apart from the fascination of finding these quaint old reminders of the early days, particularly of the seventeenth century, there are many modern stones which bear words sensitively chosen which are an inspiration. I think of the words they put on the stone of John Richard Green, the English historian: 'He died learning.' And it is hard to think of a lovelier, more telling tribute. To the end, he never lost his enthusiasm, he never ceased to enquire, and to share the shafts of wonder revealed to him. Not everyone dies learning. I would like to do that.

Another epitaph dear to me, is: 'He lighted fires in cold rooms.' I would like to do that.

And when the beloved Yorkshire writer, Winifred Holtby, died young in 1935, I was inspired by the simple, comprehensive prayer placed on her grave. It reads:

> God give me work
> Till my life shall end,
> And life
> Till my work is done.

Good News – from the Courageous

Do you ever find yourself looking back to the greatest acts of courage you know of? I do. Some are undramatic. But only this week, in the High Street of our city, I paused to consider for the first time a newly unveiled figure of Lord Bernard Freyberg, V.C., the first New Zealander to serve as our Governor. (The craftsmanship is by Anthony Stones.) Though half a world away from the setting of his rare act of courage, few of us forget it.

It was at Gallipoli, under cover of darkness, that the young officer agreed to be dropped overboard from a chosen vessel, to light decoys to encourage the enemy Turks to believe that a landing would be made in a certain area.

First, Freyberg had to be stripped, and painted black. Then he was dropped in the chill, inky waters, pushing ahead of him a raft with decoys. Guns were alerted all around him, and it was a two-hour swim. At one agreed point, he crawled through scrubby undergrowth along the shore to overhear talk from the enemy. Then, with useful information gathered, he lit his decoys; and alone, in the darkness, swam back again to his starting vessel.

Looking back on such acts, Arthur Koestler is only one of us to ask: 'What is courage? A matter of glands, nerves, conditioned by heredity and early experiences? A drop of iodine in the thyroid...?' There are many kinds, of course: brilliant action in extreme peril; a long reaction of quiet cheerfulness in pain and difficulty; a readiness to accept the beginning, without knowing what the end will be; an honesty with oneself in an unexpected situation; the courage to trust another; there is also the courage of those

116

who, when they fail, rise again, and tackle a new beginning. Not least are those in our midst – men and women (and I always like to quote a woman, when I have quoted a man) – moved by their religious faith to courageous action. They may not ever be represented by a bronze figure in the street – but God's Kingdom is pushed a little farther ahead, in the world in which life goes on today. I think of the late Bishop of Chichester, Dr George Bell; and Mother Teresa of Calcutta; of a tanker-driver whose story appeared in the newspaper, whose giant vehicle, carrying tons of nitric acid behind his cab, got out of control going down a steep hill, and who deliberately drove off the road and crashed, because he knew that at the bottom of the hill was a village. No one suffered injury – not even the courageous driver, fortunately, who managed to jump clear. There are many kinds of courage: the instantaneous; the enduring; and what I call 'the fully aware'. This, I believe, is the greatest of all.

And I have a glorious reminder of it every time I go to my coat cupboard, where hangs on the umbrella hook a Chinese umbrella – black, cheap, ordinary – with which I will never part. It was given me by my friend Annie James, a Presbyterian nurse from my country who rose to extraordinary deeds of courage for the people she served. When she came back, her shoes and garments worn to pitiful parts, this umbrella was the only whole thing she had left. But she was alive! The best energies of her years she had given to her loved Chinese people of Kaai Hau, in peace and war, through 'The Hospital of Universal Love'. The day had come when Japanese planes zoomed overhead – bombs fell, buildings were burned, and people were killed in the market. There was little that my friend and her helpers could do except gather up what they could carry – nursing mothers, babies, clothes, drugs, even the unscrewed doors of the Hospital itself. Squeaking barrows, crazy old carts, livestock, bundles of bedding, and little hoards of private belongings had all to be moved. It was a grim undertaking, and courageous!

After an interval, when the battle eased a little, the weary hospital staff tramped home. Ill-informed, little knowing the future turn of events, they screwed on their hospital doors again, and started their ministry once more. It was better than living in a broken-down, disused temple. The roadways looked like a human anthill – every living creature carried a burden. The hills called for hard climbing, but possessions left behind were all too often looted by bandits or soldiers.

But nothing remained the same for long. *Twenty times* my friend led the moving of her hospital into the hills, tending wounded soldiers and needy country people. Often rice crops were just ready to harvest when hostilities renewed themselves. Afraid to be caught gathering the grain, or mending the bridges, things were left undone, as the people fled. The only hope of life was to go again into the hills, carrying what they could. Often they knew such tiredness that they could hardly drag themselves farther. And it often happened that in the early hours of the morning an eager father, or a servant, would come hastening to the little makeshift 'hospital' for the nurse to come and 'receive life'.

Again and again, at the risk of her life and under cover of darkness, Annie climbed out-of-the-way routes over the hills to some centre where, whisperings had told her, a new supply of drugs had come. Sometimes they were perilously short, or completely used up. And at all times, of course, they had to be paid for. To manage this, the little hospital bred pigs. There was a steady market for them; but when Annie and her colleagues had to pick up things and run for the hills, they had to pick up the pigs and run with them, too. So they liked to sell them off when fairly small. They used the laundry baskets to carry them, and they prayed a lot for those pigs – lest they should squeal, in transit, and give the show away. But they never did – in all those many, and hazardous, moves!

To and fro the battle swayed. The danger to life became so great that the Consul-General wrote to Annie, instructing her to leave and come down to Kong Chuen, to Canton or Hong Kong. He pointed out that he was unable any longer to offer her any protection...

Her reply to His Britannic Majesty's Consul-General remains a diplomatic document. Such a courteous, disarming letter it was, that the Consul-General could do nothing but shrug his shoulders, turn to his secretary and say: 'Well, I can do nothing more for her, but I take off my hat to a brave woman!'

Ping Te Kong,
February 17, 1939

His Britannic Majesty's Consul-General,
Shameen, Canton.

Dear Sir,

I wish to acknowledge your letter of 1st inst., and to thank you for it. I note that you consider that it would be in the best interests of all concerned if I would vacate the Tsung Fa District.

My circumstances at the present time, however, are so different from what they were in late December when the armed robbery occurred, that I feel impelled to place these facts before you in preference to evacuating forthwith.

The conditions making my safety more secure than formerly are briefly as follows:

1. A robbery having already occurred, it is not likely to recur for many months, for the robbers realize that there is nothing left to take.

2. Robberies are always more frequent towards the Chinese New Year, so from now on things are likely to be more peaceful.
3. I have moved from the Lau Ha Wai to a district that has a much better reputation.

I have done this in consultation with the Chinese magistrate, who has taken a genuine interest in my welfare and has given special instructions to the village head and the village protection corps to guard my safety.

The temple we are in here has the protection of several men who sleep in the building at night.

I realize that only in very exceptional circumstances should a British subject pursue a course of action that is contrary to the express wishes of his Consul-General, but I feel that these exceptional circumstances exist. Thus, whilst by remaining here I am disobeying the letter of your communication of February 1st, I do not feel that I am disobeying the spirit of it; for I am sure that if you could see me in my present circumstances, and see at the same time the dire need for medical aid that exists in this district, you yourself would no longer desire my evacuation,

     I am, Sir,
       Yours respectfully,
        ANNIE JAMES

You will understand what I see here of courage – and there was more – when I had long talks with my friend and, following a request from the publishing house of her Church in New Zealand, wrote her life story in full. After a wide reading, it is now at last out of print. But I am happy to use here some of *Never A Dull Moment*, to underline my remembrance of courage. I can't forget it – I don't really need a reminder from that old Chinese umbrella in my hall cupboard.

Good News – about Words

It was the telephone ringing merrily through the house mid-morning that set me to sharing one of the privileges of my life. A new month was all but on the doorstep – Sunday would be the 2nd – and my minister would like me to read the Lessons in Church that morning.

First thing, on returning to my kindly study, I took down my Bible from its shelf to see what the chosen readings would be. But before that, my eyes fell on the beautifully-inscribed words that my Dedication Bible carried. I read: 'Presented to Sister Rita Snowden, on the occasion of her Dedication into the Order of Deaconesses in the Methodist Church of New Zealand.' Then followed the signature of the President of the Church Conference; and that of the Secretary; and that of the Superintendent of Methodist Deaconess House; and it bore the date March 2nd, 1930. So it was exactly fifty years, to the day, since the Church first put that book into my hands. (My minister had no idea of it, though I told him when I went into the vestry; and he told the congregation later, when I stepped up to the lectern to read.)

Dr Richard Green Moulton used to say: 'Whatever other uses men may wish to make of the Bible, our first and paramount duty *is to read it.*' I think he might more aptly have used the word 'privilege' than 'duty', although for years I read my Bible as a task enjoined, rather than a delight to be enjoyed. Then I came across Dr Anthony Deane's little book: *How to Enjoy the Bible.* It was a revelation to me – and I entered into that great library, that I had made the mistake of approaching as *one book* – with folk-stories belonging to the childhood of the race, history, poetry, drama, love lyrics, biography, gospels, and letters, etc. Plainly, these had each to be read differently. And this I confirmed later, as a student in training, since it applied not only to reading in private, *but to reading in public.*

How seldom, it seems – listening intently to those who rise to read in church, is this point honoured – and it is an essential point.

And there are others which, grasped clearly – as our old chaplain required in lecture time, and from the lectern on Sundays – that can greatly enliven the whole.

First, I have always taken time carefully to read over the chosen passage beforehand, so that I may know the mood of it, and its exact meaning. (Sometimes, there is even a pronunciation to become sure of. I cannot count, looking back, on how many occasions – when a lay-person has come forward to read as part of the Service of Worship – this has not been done.)

Needless to add, there is need at the outset to decide which version of the Bible to use. The Authorized Version (as is my Dedication Bible) is without doubt the most beautiful, the chief glory of English prose. 'Through three centuries,' as Dr Anthony Deane says, 'no other work has had a comparable influence on our creed and thought, on our speech and literature.' Now and again we hear someone say: 'The Bible means little to me – except that I find it what some claim for it: "magnificent literature".' Dr C.S. Lewis, in our day, has a telling answer for these: 'Those who read the Bible *as literature only*, do not read the Bible – *it is a religious book.*'

When I am to read in public, I check the chosen passage in each of my several versions, and use the familiar Authorized Version when the reading is precious to many of my listeners for such passages as the Christmas Story in Luke 2: 'And it came to pass in those days, that there went out a decree from Caesar Augustus . . . And there were in the same country shepherds abiding in the field, keeping watch over their flock by night...' going on to 'Glory to God in the highest, and on earth peace, good will toward men.' And there are many other favourite passages: the 8th Psalm; the 23rd Psalm; the 24th Psalm; Isaiah 9; Isaiah 40; and even more in the New Testament: John 14; Romans 8; and the Love passage from chapter 13 of St Paul's first letter to the Corinthians: 'Though I speak with the tongues of men and of angels...' ending so gloriously: 'Now abideth faith, hope, charity, these three; but the greatest of these is charity.' (Though this, I find myself admitting, is one passage that does profit from being read in the Moffatt Version or the Revised Standard Version. 'So faith, hope, *love* abide, these three; but the greatest of these is *love*.' 'Charity' is an old word that now carries a different meaning. The reading of the Bible is not just a pleasant exercise, or an action of merit in itself – its message has to be received for what it is, and to be relevant.)

When that revered leader, Bishop Berggrav, Primate of Norway, was imprisoned, the chief of police said to him: 'You may write to your wife one letter a week.' On the first Sunday in Advent 1942 he wrote in his letter to her: 'I have been reading the Gospel for the day. It says: "He hath anointed me to proclaim release to the captives."' The chief of police sent for the bishop's wife – the letter had been censored. 'Your husband must not discuss current affairs in his letters,' said he, 'nor must he quote the Bible – *it is far too topical.*'

But would one think this was accepted as so by many to whom the Bible is read Sunday by Sunday? I have checked this reaction, over many years, in many parts of the world. Attention all too often lags; a glassy look comes over the eyes of those listening, or pretending to listen. The first time I began to think about it, I felt obliged to own my share of responsibility, and tried to do something about it.

And I find no moment of my Christian witness more thrilling than that when, in reading, I can get all eyes toward me, all worshippers listening to every word. So one goes over the passage beforehand to decide which words in each sentence call for emphasis, even underlining them on the page. This helps the whole to carry its full meaning, lifting it from a grey commonplace to give it a royal shine. It is a thousand pities that such care ever lags.

One with much experience writes in *The Methodist Recorder* for us: 'Family services are immensely popular, and attract large congregations. They occasionally have one ingredient – though this does not only apply to "Family Services" – about which I feel more than a vague disquiet. I refer', says this columnist, '*to the incompetent reading of the Lessons by the unpractised.*'

'There are,' I am glad to have him add, 'some lay men and women who are so much better at it than the average clergyman, that if I were one of these, I would be ashamed to read the Lesson in church again, until I had mastered the art.' For good reading is an art. He is not, he makes plain, asking for an elocutionary effort, or what he calls 'a histrionic theatricality' – and I should hope not.

Many common words at the time when our Authorized Version made its entry into the world no longer carry their original meanings, which is reason enough for using a modern version. (The word 'Comfort', for example, has nothing to do with cushioned ease. In those days, when my Dedication AV Bible was translated, it meant 'strengthen', and carried a challenge, as did the entry of Bishop Asbury, pioneer of the Methodist Church in America, centuries nearer our time, in concluding a section of his famous *Journal*: 'Our Conference ended on Friday, with a *comfortable* intercession.' The word 'Coasts' in 1611, the year when our much-prized AV was printed, were boundaries, but not necessarily made by the sea. And the word 'lust' meant strong desire, but not necessarily of a sexual nature. And, as is more widely known, the word 'cunning' meant a very different thing from what we mean when we come across it in our paperback detective yarns. It meant *skill*, as in the Psalmist's longing: 'If I forget thee, O Jerusalem, let my right hand forget her cunning.')

Finally, it is good, in my experience, not only to underline those few words that need emphasis, but also the places where pauses can be effective. Holding these points in mind, as a general habit, one can soon be at ease before a congregation.

One more point is a postscript: it is surprisingly few who arrive at ease, who do learn to breathe well as they approach the task, for the benefit not only of the deaf and the distant worshippers, but for the pleasant, clear hearing of all, when one holds his or her Bible, so that there is no looking-down at the lectern. One's voice travels to the back of the building, that way.

One gets inspiration from a listening congregation. Lately, I had the privilege of reading at a crowded Ecumenical Service in our Cathedral. And many people unknown to me approached me on leaving, with the simple statement: 'I heard every word.' (There ought to be nothing remarkable about that.)

I find myself, on such occasions, silently borrowing Joseph Conrad's preface to one of his books: 'My task ... is by the power of the human word, to make you hear, to make you feel ... to make you see.'

Yes, it is to join in Worship!

Good News – of the Second Half

It often happens that one gets only half a truth, even in church, although it is not an intentional denial. And Paul's words are good teaching in our growth in stewardship: 'God loveth a cheerful giver' (2 Corinthians 9:7, AV). From childhood up, many of us are liable to hold too closely what is our own – a worn teddy-bear, a bag of bright marbles, a storybook, a coin from a moneybox slithered out with the aid of a dinner knife. We have to learn to give, and to some it comes easier than to others.

But it is only half the truth! Paul might have coined another statement every bit as true, though he did not: 'God loveth a cheerful receiver.' This, like the first meeting with the first saying, involves not only toys, material things, and coins, but gifts of personality, gifts of spirit, gifts of time itself. All the way through the New Testament, this balance is implied, if not exactly stated. We have each to think it out, and apply it for ourselves. Early in my twenties, I awakened to a desire to write, as part of my stewardship. And one day, I came across an English journal with an advertisement that caught my eye, telling of a course that offered the very help that I needed. Out of my modest savings, I straightway sent off to London for it.

After some months – since mails by surface were slow – the first set of instructions arrived. But after such an interval, I was no longer free to give time to a correspondence course, so I wrote off to the promoters in London, explaining things. Soon, since I had paid for it, the total set of lessons arrived, but after a quick look, I stowed them away in a cupboard. Weeks and months went by when, suffering from a protracted heart condition, I had to depend on help from others, help with weeding and lawn-cutting and other chores.

I was grateful to a young friend who came in to help with one or two tasks. I knew that Tony loved books, but one day he chanced to speak of a great desire he had to learn to write, and all of a sudden, I fell to thinking of my set of lessons in the cupboard. I did not mention them then, but later I made up my mind to give them to Tony, although, of course, the time had lapsed for any professional comment. But I felt sure the course would start my young friend upon his way.

I was utterly astonished on his next visit, to find that what I so eagerly offered, *he would not receive.* I urged him as best I knew how, holding out the printed course, brought from the cupboard, with the words: 'It is not being used. If you don't use it, it will be wasted – and I have a conscience about all the pounds I spent on it.'

'No,' was his answer, 'I cannot take it – it represents too much money.'

When he had gone, I set myself to think out other approaches, but it was no use, and Tony never did carry off that course on writing – *he just couldn't let himself receive it*! I had never before felt so utterly frustrated, so defeated. And there was nothing more that I could do.

From that day on, I saw how *giving and receiving were but two parts of a whole*! Even God is powerless to give us what He would if we will not receive His gift, even His Gracious Son, in time on this earth. (The saddest verse in the whole New Testament, I feel, is John 1:11, AV: 'He came unto His own, *and His own received Him not.*')

Some time after the war was at an end, I was a guest in a Dutch home. We sat, when it came to dinner, with Father and Mother at each end of the table, their guest and large family between them. During the worst of those dragging, hungry years, Father – now at the head of the table – had gone often into known country parts to find something extra to eat. At the lowest level of their hunger, they had even eaten leaves; and more than once, almost home, he had been brazenly relieved of his finds by the enemy occupier.

I was now movingly aware of all this, when the Grace at table had been said. Then, the first serving from the minute joint came down the long table to me. At that moment, the Father spoke: 'It is a small portion,' said he to me, 'but it comes from a large heart.' (I was from the other side of the world, where we had had enough to eat, for all that some items were restricted. During the whole of wartime, I had never gone hungry, never lacked meat. In the fraction of time it took for that slender serving to come down the table to me, I questioned myself about receiving it – a meal of meat meant less to me than to others at that table.) Mercifully, I realized something of the family's planning, and giving, to serve such a meal to their guest. Without anyone being aware of my decision, I made a meaningful act of Receiving. It was utterly fitting – it was even sacramental: the wholeness of Giving and Receiving!

Would that on all occasions of relationship, we could respond as naturally.

Some time ago, our newspapers carried news of Prince Philip, on a visit to Mexico to meet the people of that country. And there, he was delighted to meet one very special Mexican – not an official of government, nor a rich merchant, a gifted artist, a craftsman, but a little girl. And that day she reminded the Prince, and all who shared the day with them, of the beautiful secret of giving and receiving. In her charming photograph, she looked about four years of age, and she had come from a children's centre in Guadalajara City.

At a certain moment she was lifted up to be greeted by the Prince, and he gave her a kiss, as a special gesture. Her reaction was to give him two outsize daisies – with shortish stems, as most little girls' flowers picked from a garden, seem to have.

Prince Philip received them royally, though they were much too big to put in his buttonhole. What then did he do with them? *He carried them around with him* all the rest of that day; and every photograph taken of the royal visitor showed those two outsize daisies!

It is a curious thing that in church we hear much more about the art of giving, than the art of receiving – yet they belong together. Few things are more wounding in this world, than to have a gift refused. To receive with love and satisfaction is proof of a royal spirit!

Allen Birtwhistle is another of our day who believes that we would be immensely richer if we would gladly grasp this secret. 'It may be', he says, 'that the final law of the universe is neither a simple *Offer* nor *Demand*, but *Give* and *Take* ... It does not seem to be contrary to the spirit of our Lord to suggest that there are times when it is *more gracious, more humble to receive than to give.* It may be that sometimes the only right thing to do is to allow someone to gird himself with a towel and kneel down and wash your feet.'

Good News – of Joy

I have known for a long time now that Joy and Jollity were
not the same, but never till today have I given my
well-worn Oxford Dictionary a chance to tell me that they
are 'a whole page apart'. *Joy* is plainly a matter of heart,
of spirit; whilst *Jollity* is a lighter thing altogether. The
Dictionary is satisfied to spin it out in two words:
'merrymaking, festivity'.

The word 'Jollity' doesn't qualify for a single mention
in my New Testament; whereas in that Book of Life so
close to life, 'Joy', 'Great Joy', and 'Joyful' are there
more than a hundred and sixty times.

They have a special place in the unravelling of God's
glorious purpose in the coming of Christ. Joy is the
essential spirit of the Incarnation. To this end, God sought
the self-giving of the young woman, Mary, busy about her
household tasks. Let into His secret, Mary was at first
afraid, but soon her fear left her, and she replied, in
suitable spirit: 'Behold, the handmaid of the Lord: be it
unto me according to Thy word.' Soon she set off across
country, to visit her relative Elisabeth, also in the same
great plan, chosen to be the mother of Jesus's forerunner,
John the Baptist. Their fear overcome, they shared their
God-given status, *with Joy*! Elisabeth, no longer young,
found words to say to youthful Mary: 'Whence is this to
me, that the mother of my Lord should come to me?' For
lo, the record says, 'as soon as the voice of salutation
sounded in mine ears, the Babe leaped in my womb for
Joy!' (Luke 1:35–44, AV).

The allotted nine months of womanly patience passed
for both; and then to a little huddle of humble shepherds

out under the stars, watching their sheep, an angel messenger came, saying: 'Fear not! For, behold, I bring you *good tidings of great Joy*, which shall be to all people. For unto you is born this day in the city of David a Saviour, which is Christ the Lord. And this shall be a sign unto you; ye shall find the Babe wrapped in swaddling-clothes, lying in a manger!' And this message was enshrined, not in the steadily marching words of a sermon, but in the leaping and dancing joy of song! To grow up to be the most joyous personality to be known on God's earth! Those who paint solemn pictures of Him, and call Him all the time, 'the Man of Sorrows', know but half the truth. He is also '*the Man of Joy!*'

He commenced His public ministry at a village wedding in Cana of Galilee where, being a bridal party, they were not required by the Law to fast. 'We are as a bridal party', He said, and those sharing that happy occasion knew what He meant, but they must have been greatly surprised to find Him making use of that setting in which to start His God-called ministry.

And when He gathered about Him His handful of disciples, with the so soon shadow of the Cross over His way, as He underlined for them the lasting realities, He spoke of *His Joy*! They already knew of His joy as a village lad, running with others, about the hills, the wind in their hair. And in His teaching, whilst with them – their young Master and Lord – He had referred to *His Joy in people, and in creatures*. He found in Nature, walking the field paths on their way from village to village, from town to city, the insignificant sparrows that seemed of such little value; and the wild flowers that hung over their sandals as they proceeded along the narrow paths; and there were joys of Nature that they learned, as they slept at night under the stars, comforted only by a diminishing campfire. But together they came to know a deeper, unquenchable Joy, in sharing a rare, hitherto-unknown

131

fellowship, hammered out of their utter trust in God. In that Upper Room, where they shared the Last Supper, and there wasn't much time left, He graciously underlined it: 'As the Father hath loved Me, so have I loved you; continue ye in My love. If ye keep My commandments, ye shall abide in My love; even as I have kept My Father's commandments, and abide in His love. *These things have I spoken unto you, that My Joy might remain in you, and that your Joy might be full!*' (John 15:9–11, AV).

His arrest came; His humiliating, unjust judgement; the sweaty, burdensome carrying of the Cross out to the cruel hilltop of crucifixion; the faithfulness of a few; the gentle burial of His body in a borrowed tomb never yet used by man. But three lonely, sad days later, He was with them again – risen from the dead! And after appearing amidst them here and there for a good length of days, 'He led them out as far as Bethany, and He lifted up His hands and blessed them. And it came to pass, while He blessed them, He was parted from them, and carried up into heaven. And they worshipped Him' (and then follows a most surprising word; for they might have been utterly sorrow-ful and cast-down at their separation. But no! For they believed that it was only a *physical* separation, and that His loving, supreme, spiritual Presence would continue with them, and without any of the earth-born limitations to which they had been subject.) So, surprisingly, the record (Luke 24, second-to-last verse, in this loved gospel) says: 'They worshipped Him, and *returned to Jerusalem with great Joy.*'

Did any handful of friends, up until that time, ever return from parting with a dear friend, with Joy? If any of us, today, return with a similar spirit from a graveyard or crematorium, surely it is only for His sake. His assured Risen Presence, beyond Death, makes all the differ-ence!

Underlining this glorious word, that Jesus daily wove

into His experience here, on our earth, my scholarly friend, the late Dr William Barclay, took pleasure in reminding us that the Greek word for 'Joy' is *chara*, with its basis in religion, having its foundation in the dependable character of God. 'It is not,' he adds, 'the joy that comes from earthly things, or cheap triumphs; still less is it a joy that comes from triumphing over someone else in rivalry or competition.'

During one overshadowed period of His life, our Lord had to say, as realistically as He chose always to speak: 'Ye therefore now have sorrow; but I will see you again, and your heart shall rejoice, *and your Joy no man taketh away from you*' (John 16:22, AV).

This striking saying comes ringing down the years to us, one by one; there is no escaping sorrow – if it could be done by faith, religion would become an insurance policy, it would pay one. Unearned good comes, and unearned ill.

The kind of Joy that our Lord offers to us one by one still, by faith, is not the outcome of propitious circumstances; nor is it at the mercy of things that can happen. Some of the most joyous Christians in our world today are handicapped people, or valiant souls imprisoned for their witness in cruel countries. In his day, when the Church was young in the world, Paul was lashed by strong interpreters of the law; thrown out of a town where he was preaching; shut up in one dreary prison after another; not to mention his dragging experience of bodily trial that he called his '*thorn in the flesh.*' *But the New Testament epistle to the Philippians, that has been fittingly called The Epistle of Joy*, came from his pen, or was dictated by him when his right hand was in shackles. Despite its brevity – but four chapters, which can be rapidly read – the word 'Joy' and 'Rejoice' occur within it no less than fifteen times! Not only does it speak his own secret of living triumph, but it is something essentially Christian that he

133

wants to share. The New English Bible, translated in our generation, makes it sound like a wedding telegram, or a glorious Christmas greeting, sped on its way to one's dearly loved: '*I wish you all Joy in the Lord. I will say it again: all Joy be yours!*'

Paul knew, every bit as clearly as did Dr Harry Fosdick, writing of 'The Master's Joy', in our time, that 'Jesus was so joyful in His friendships, and His work, that He fairly was forced to defend Himself, on account of it. What some of His enemies in temple, synagogue and state whispered was a gross slander – even if they had never before happened upon a religious teacher with His secret spirit. The truth was, there had never before lived on earth, to move amongst people and creatures, such a Teacher!'

If we have not found Joy as He offers it, it could be that we have not, like those of early days, been spending enough time in His company. Or pouring out our best gifts and energies in His service! '*We Christians*', said the beloved world Church leader, Dr Hendrik Kramer, a few years ago, when he came out of concentration camp, '*must get the Joy of Christ back into our religion. We are denying Him, all too often!*'

Centred on God, His Father, His Joy manifested itself naturally, and daily, in unexpected ways. He drew little children to Himself – a sure test, since little ones will have nothing to do with a sullen grownup. His Joy lightened with expectation the sick, and the sad; it attracted the sinner, and accepted her ointment of spikenard, poured over His feet, that she might go on her way forgiven. He saw Matthew seated at his thankless job of tax gathering, and called him to a better expenditure of his energies; it lightened up the hospitality of Mary and Martha, and led them into hope of the resurrection, when Lazarus died. Centred around his burial place, they needed Joy. And in that land, then, there were countless others – and though we live far from Palestine, there still are!

His deep energizing Joy can renew and enrich in a hundred ways! Looking back with wonder to any one setting that allowed Him to express His Joy, I can only say . . .

> . . . A city drew Him,
> Flowers He found in little children's eyes;
> Something of grace in lepers stumbling to Him;
> Fragrance from spikenard spilt in glad surprise;
> *JOY in forgiving men*, at last, who slew Him.

(Anon)

*   *   *

Countless men and women, set in commonplace circumstances like ourselves, have been as glad to recall as much. And to this hour, we, in our time and setting, borrow the beloved Bernard of Clairvaux's hymn to express our prayer:

> *Jesus, Thou Joy of loving hearts,*
>   Thou Fount of life, Thou Light of men,
> From the best bliss that earth imparts
>   We turn unfilled to Thee again.
>
> Thy truth unchanged hath ever stood;
>   Thou savest them that on Thee call;
> To them that seek Thee Thou art good,
>   To them that find Thee, all in all!

Good News – from Good Followers

I hushed my heart! The early morning light was on Galilee's clear waters; creases in the gentle surrounding hills. Below me worked local fishermen, browned, companionable, busy at their nets – they might have been Peter, Andrew and company, little seemed to have changed. On this very shore, under these very skies, One passing had stopped to issue a unique call: '*Follow Me!*'

In actuality it was long ago now, and, one by one, each had made his own response, not on the outer rim of life, but at its heart. Dr William Barclay was to put it well: 'It is not to be thought that on this day for the first time He stood before them. No doubt they had stood in the crowd and listened; no doubt they had stayed to talk long after the rest of the crowd had drifted away. No doubt they already had felt the magic of His presence and the magnetism of His eyes. But Jesus did not say to them, "I have a theological system which I would like you to investigate; I have certain theories that I would like you to think over; I have an ethical system I would like to discuss with you."

'He said: "Follow Me!" It all began with a personal reaction to Himself; it all began in that tug of the heart which begets the unshakable loyalty. (This is not to say that there are none who *think* themselves into Christianity; but it is to say that for most of us following Christ is like falling in love.) It has been said that "we admire people for reasons; we love them without reasons". The thing happens just because they are they, and we are we . . . In by far the greatest number of cases a man

136

follows Jesus Christ, not because of anything that Jesus said, but because of *everything that Jesus is!*'

He did not say: 'Understand Me!' – it was only as they followed, beginning their adventures there in Galilee, that some knowledge of Him came: as the Son of God, and Brother of men, setting up an everlasting Kingdom. And they did not understand all that there was to know, even when they had been with Him a long time, tramping the dusty paths between village and village, with occasional visits to the city, speaking to the crowds; healing the sick; sleeping often, at day's end, camp-style out under the stars; finding what human comfort they could round a little fire.

One day, as they continued to follow, He put a surprising question to them: 'Whom do men say that I, the Son of Man, am?' (Matthew 16:13, AV). It was a surprising question at that stage. I can see a good many eyebrows go up. 'And they said, "Some say that thou art John the Baptist; some say Elias; and others, Jeremias, or one of the prophets."' Then came the question with the greatest crunch in it: 'He saith unto them, *But whom say ye that I am?*' It was only then that Simon Peter came out with his ageless statement: '*Thou art the Christ, the Son of the Living God!*' (Matthew 16:16, AV).

Some time had elapsed, and they were learning all the time, as they followed. 'But He did not even then' – as Dr Colin Morris, distinguished Methodist preacher of our day, administrator, and servant of the BBC, reminds us – 'ask them to pray to Him, sing about Him, or even worship Him.' His only call – and as I stood, heart-hushed, that morning by Galilee, it seemed so simple, so straightforward – was 'Follow Me!'

But, of course, it's not just so simple in our day to follow Him. Whoever claimed as much – it never was! Now, as one writes, for each one of us as we face Him, a question arises:

Dim tracts of Time divide
Those golden days from me;
Thy voice comes strange o'er years of change;
How can we follow Thee?

Your response, and mine, can't be a geographical, literal
following, like that which Peter, James and Andrew and
the other fishermen of Galilee made, step by step, through
the dusty tracks into the villages.

It's not even a reverential looking back to that first
Christian century: it's a laying hold of a reality of
relationship here and now – and on into the future. Dr
George Matheson, the beloved Scottish minister who gave
us the moving hymn 'O Love that wilt not let me go' knew
what it involved: not only 'a Love that would not let one
go', but also 'a Love that would not let one off'. Said he,
in simple day-to-day prose, when he was aspiring to
poetry of the soul: 'Son of Man, whenever I doubt, I think
of Thee ... Thou never growest old to me. Last century
is old, last season is obsolete. *Thou art abreast of all the
centuries*; nay, Thou goest before them like a star. I have
never come up with Thee, modern as I am.'

This is the wonder that another close to my own heart
has put into a neat verse, that once gave me a title
Adventuring Still.

He goes adventuring still
Who slipt the hold of Time.

And I marvel at what that continues to mean. It means that
that wonderful character Who walked the rim of Galilee
and, talking with fellowmen, called them to follow, was
not limited – *but dealing with issues belonging to God's
Kingdom of values, beyond Time*. On the dusty ways of
Galilee, and the little of earth's geography that He knew
– and to cover Palestine today, north, south, east and

west, as I have done, is to know how very small it was –
the time had to come, as it did come, when He had to say
to His disciples: 'It is expedient for you that I go away'
(John 16:7, AV). (There were places He could never be in
when desperately needed, because He was limited to a
human body, respecting Time, and could be in only one
at a time. There must have been many homes into which
He could have gone as a guest, beside that of Lazarus,
Mary and Martha in Bethany: Peter the fisherman's
lake-side home was one, and a handful of others. But He
couldn't – He was limited. There must have been many
other blind beggars besides Bartimaeus, hour after hour
in his darkness, waiting for Jesus to come that way. But
He was limited, until after His Death He gave up Time
altogether, with His Resurrection, and returned to the
Father. Only then could He say, and with wondrous
confidence and joy: 'All power is given unto Me in heaven
and earth . . . and lo, I am with you always, even unto the
end of the world' (Matthew 28:18–20, AV).

And those first disciples, as well as those added to their
number, although having to part with the dear bodily
presence of their Master, did not come back to their daily
setting with grief – but 'with joy', as the New Testament
reminds us. And men and women like you and me, have
found ever since, the world over, what His spiritual
presence means: He has exchanged the *limited centre* for
the *world circumference*, the *occasional presence for the
continual presence*! (How kind He was – had they but
known it at the time – to underline for them this wonderful
reality: 'It is expedient for you that I go away!' Without
that, we Christians would all have to go on literal
pilgrimage to where He was said to be – an even greater
impossibility now than when He was in little Palestine.)

Now we have, by faith, to deal with a Lord and Master
Who knows no limitations, Who 'goes adventuring still' –
and we with Him! It's a wonderful modern-day truth about

139

discipleship. We followers of Jesus have no reason to 'browse along with heads down, nibbling at a few little ideas'. We are sharing in a great adventure – and with the Greatest Adventurer of all Time and Eternity!

Dr David L. Edwards, in his book *A Reason to Hope*, underlines this confidently: 'It now appears that the greatest mistake which Christians could commit would be to believe that the activity of God has been exhausted by the creation of the universe as it now is, or by the evolution of man in his present condition, or by the work of the founders of the great religions, *or by the work of Jesus, or by Christianity in its first two thousand years.* Scientists expect this planet to be inhabitable for another two or three thousand million years at least, unless man first makes it uninhabitable. The story of agriculture, now only ten thousand years old, is surely going to produce some new developments in that future, as is the six-thousand-year-old story of civilization or the four-hundred-year-old story of science or the two-hundred-year-old story of industry. *But the same reasoning suggests, particularly to a Christian, that the story of Christianity is not yet ended!*'

Good News – about Passports

Do you ever, in a quiet place, or on a solitary rail journey or a long flight, ask yourself: 'What kind of person am I?'

One thing is certain, if you are on your way to some distant place, to share the beauty, the mystery and pleasantness of life there, it's only possible if you carry on your person 'a valuable document' which answers some basic questions. Customs authorities, in whatever country you find yourself, are insistent on this.

So I fill in my papers, before I set off, as part of my preparations for travel. I give my full name, in capitals, and place of birth, and date. I give my height, and other physical details – the colour of my hair, my eyes; any marks (a mole, for instance, or a scar on my chin). And I must declare my profession. Several copies of a recent small 'head-and-shoulders' photograph are essential, one of which will be pasted into my completed passport. Then, before it is officially handed over to me, a number will be punched through its cover. At that point, as I respectfully take my leave, I am immediately faced with the need to decide on the handiest, safest place in which to keep it, so that I shall be able to present it without fuss at the Customs barrier at the port, airport or frontier where I find myself.

From time to time, alas, there appears a sprinkling of 'doubtful', even 'deceitful', travellers. They have themselves prepared a phoney passport, or bought one from the black market in some back street, and they hope to get away with it, aided by its contrived photograph. (Though it is true that there are, among us travellers of unquestioned honesty, some who don't take a good photograph, but we can't do much about it. Of these, Sir John Hunt, leader of the famous Everest Expedition, says with a chuckle: 'If most of us are as sick as we look in our photographs in our passports, then we are too sick to travel, and ought to stay at home!')

I can name at least one famous and widely experienced traveller of our day, who neither desires to cheat nor would be able to do so. Not only does his passport carry an excellent photograph, but it is stamped 'Number One'. He is the Duke of Edinburgh, and his profession is filled in as 'Prince of the Royal House'.

Passports, I am led to believe, go back to King Canute of the eleventh century, who is credited with being the first to issue such an essential document. It was prepared for pilgrims travelling to the tombs of St Peter and of St Paul, in Rome. (A copy extant begins with the name of the personage granting it: 'I, to our holy and apostolic and venerable father in Christ, and to all kings, bishops, abbots, priests and clerks in every nation of Christendom, who devote themselves to the service of the Creator, in monasteries, in cities, in villages, or in hamlets. Be it known to you that this our brother [the bearer of the passport] and your servant, has obtained permission from us to proceed on a pilgrimage to the Church of Saint Peter, your father, and to other churches, to pray for his soul's sake, for yours and for ours.

'Therefore do we address this to you, begging that you will, for the love of God and of Saint Peter, give him hospitable treatment, aiding, consoling, and comforting him – affording him free ingress, egress and regress, so that he may in safety return to us . . .') An impressive document!

Relationships are even more involved these days, and we have an increasing need for identification, when so many more of us continually travel. The issuing of passports has reached an all-time level. (I never even saw one in my twenties.) Linking people together for mutual good, a passport today has also a peculiar power of assuring one of individuality.

I remember once, in my student years, overhearing two people whom I knew slightly speaking of these matters. One, with longing in her voice, said: 'I wish I could be So-and-So!' The instant response from her companion was: 'I wish you could be yourself!' I remained silent; but thereafter I have often found myself murmuring a rhyme I picked up:

> I never can hide myself from ME;
> I see what others can never see;
> I know what others can never know;
> I have to live with myself, and so
> I want to be fit for myself to know!

Passports cannot be alike, any more than personalities. How dull our world would be if they were! I marvel at the diversity shown by the Creator: two eyes, a nose, and a mouth each – and no two exactly alike. This strikes me whenever I find myself in a crowd in some great city of this world.

When our Master chose His first disciples, each was very different. No one of them had quite the nature of another. Peter, the rough fisherman, was a fellow bronzed by the sun and sea air, impulsive, ready always with a word. Andrew his brother was a lot less sure of himself, less talkative, a 'background man'. And there was John, blessed with the scholar's mind and sensitive spirit. Philip was different again, with a spate of questions when the hungry thousands gathered about the Master, far from any city or village source of supplies. His question was very much to the point: 'Where shall we buy bread that these may eat?' And Thomas – to introduce in this individual way no more of that amazing Twelve – was a man of doubts. And the New Testament record shows us them in their various manifestations, working up to the words of his disciple friends, when Jesus had risen. Thomas was absent; and when he returned they came spilling over with what was *wonderful good news* – and to Thomas, unbelievable! 'On the evening of that day [the first day of the week] the doors being shut where the disciples were for fear of the Jews, Jesus came and stood among them, and said to them, "Peace be with you". When he had said this, he showed them his hands and his side. Then the disciples were glad when they saw the Lord. Jesus said to them again, "Peace be with you. As the Father has sent me, even so I send you" ... Now Thomas, one of the twelve, called the Twin, was not with them when Jesus came. So the other disciples told him, "We have seen the Lord".

'But he said to them, "Unless I see in His hands the print of the nails, and place my finger in the mark of the nails, and place my hand in His side, I will not believe."'

And Jesus met Thomas, at the point of his doubt. 'Eight days later', the New Testament says, 'his disciples were again in the house, and Thomas was with them. The doors were shut, but Jesus came and stood among them, and said, 'Peace be with you'. Then he said to Thomas, 'Put your finger here, and see My hands; and put out your hand, and place it in My side – do not be faithless, but believing.' Thomas answered him, '*My Lord and my God!*' (John 20:19–28,RSV).

And there were the women, also of that warm loyalty: Martha, and her sister Mary; Mary the mother of James and Joses; and the mother of Zebedee's children. And with the passage of time came others. Priscilla, wife of Aquila – opening their home to travelling Christians, supporting them in fellowship; and Dorcas, the needle-woman of Joppa, 'full of good works, and alms deeds', as some chose to describe her. And all through the centuries, to this day, there have been others. Of some, we have read; and the names and deeds of others are known to us, some, even in our own locality, alive to this day.

A short time ago, a new sign – with a blue background, and some striking words – was set up in front of Wesley Church, Taranaki Street, in our capital city. I knew the young woman artist responsible for setting it out so artistically and appealingly; and I knew the minister responsible for having it raised there, having sat under his chairmanship on a literary committee. I wrote asking his permission to pass on its message in this book.

For its wording – in this age of hurrying masses – speaks to me clearly, like the spirit of my passport: '*We believe every man is special and of value.*'

This might well be realized by members of the Church who step up off the passing street to worship there, but there are also the casual passers-by. This conviction so tellingly stated is an essential, if the life given us by God is to be Good! In a whole day's gathering of News, there can be nothing more revolutionary. God does not care *only* for totals, masses, hurrying crowds going goodness knows where – *He cares for you, and for me, and just where we are.*

And isn't this the kind of Good News that makes Life interesting 'in this wide world'?

Good News – about Nicknames

I don't know how I did it, but somehow I got all the way through my schooldays and up to my valedictionary service as an adult student, without a nickname. If you want to be unkind, you can suggest that I must have been a colourless character. I can't argue. I can only say that to me my growing up seemed anything but colourless, with laughter and learning, playingfields, gracious trees and wide skies our daily setting. We had nicknames amongst us, such as 'Sparkie', immediately off the mark at cricket; at the other extreme 'Fatty' – a languid classmate who spent all her small pocketmoney on penny creamcakes.

In time, I was ready to step out into the great world. Only then did I get my nickname, 'Snowie', from a play on my family name. But I did not mind it; and many of my closest friends use it to this day. It has kept alive my interest in nicknames.

Years on, I walked into the Scottish border-town of Melrose, carrying my haversack and my travelling eagerness. Like many another, I had been drawn to the town by a lovely magazine photograph of its silhouetted Abbey ruins. I had no idea that there I would come upon a young woman's nickname, 'Sunshine', that I've never forgotten. Nor could I imagine that her full name, Elizabeth Clephane, was already in the hymnbook that I used Sunday by Sunday. True, the two hymns that she gave to the world have dated a little with the years, although many a one like myself has gained something from them, at some stage of adulthood. The first – about the good shepherd – begins: 'There were ninety-and-nine that safely lay in the shelter of the fold . . .' (Matthew 18:12–14,

AV). The other called for an even more serious responsiveness, and began: 'Beneath the Cross of Jesus, I fain would take my stand...' Though I have not been called to sing either for some time, it was good to recall them there in Melrose, where their author had answered to the lively nickname 'Sunshine'.

* * *

I went some time later, on another first time visit, to the small Staffordshire town of Walsall, sent there by my London publishers on a speaking engagement. And there I came upon another nickname. Dorothy Pattison was a highly spirited member of a minister's large family. Her father's mental aberrations caused him many worries about how they would all grow up; but he needn't have worried – least of all about Dorothy. In the conflicting currents of growing up, nobody now knows how, or when, she got her name 'Dora', or, more strictly, her nickname.

Their mother was in poor health, too, and early in the home setting Dora, as she was called, had a first taste of the satisfaction of nursing somebody back to health. It persevered beyond the time when she was engaged to serve as a village schoolmistress. She soon captured the children's interest and love. 'But,' said one onlooker who knew her well, 'it always seemed to us evident that she was called, from a child, to the work to which she was eventually led.' And that was true. No task was beneath her dignity. Middle-class visitors were 'astonished', to use their words, to find Miss Pattison blacking her own grate. But she was to do many more humble tasks, in the years to come, under the wide necessity of nursing.

For nursing was her true vocation. At first, her teaching behind her, she joined an Anglican Order of women, and as a novice applied herself to utter learning and serving.

147

As 'Sister Dora', she earned the love and friendship of many of the needy, sick and shabby.

And in time, with courageous spirit and nursing competence, she moved from the North Ormesby Cottage Hospital, on to Coatham Convalescent Home, on to the Walsall Cottage Hospital where, undiminished to this day, her name shines gloriously. She was the essence of love, humility, joy. Walsall, from the beginning of her service, was on the grim border of the Black Country, where were many coalmines and blast furnaces. So that, added to fever visitations, and sicknesses of a lesser kind, were many grave accidents. Sister Dora was soon undertaking operations, as well as journeys to tend outpatients. When these outmatched the time she had to spend on them, not to speak of the strength, the local railway men, out of gratitude for her service to themselves and their families, collected among themselves bit by bit the considerable sum of fifty pounds, and bought her a little pony and carriage.

At the close of her long days in hospital, and around among the people, she was still on call at night. Above her pillow she hung a little bell, with the inscription from the New Testament: '*The Master is come, and calleth for thee*' – words spoken to the sisters of Bethany, Mary and Martha, when their brother died (John 11:28, AV). Dora liked to remind herself that the call of the needy of Walsall, at any hour of the day or night, was, in very truth, the call of Christ. And she rose at once, and, however tired, ministered to them.

To some of her longtime inpatients she gave whimsical nicknames, which eased their long hours' patience: 'Mr Head', 'Mr Thumb', 'Darky', 'King Charles'. One of her patients, an old Irish bricklayer, is remembered to have said of her: 'Sure, an' isn't Sister Dora like the blessed saints? One look, and she told me I was a builder!' When passed on to the loved head of the Hospital, she smiled enjoyably and said: 'Well, his clothes were full of dust, he smelled of mortar, and I had just taken a piece of brick out of his eye – so it was hardly remarkable!' But there were things that were remarkable, in the operations that she saw through; the fright of little children whom she took up in her arms, and brought to peace; the rough men and anxious women, who alike put their complete trust in Sister Dora. She was 'theirs' in a way that no one else ever was. And in her death she was 'theirs', too – and not only on the day when they gathered to give thanks to God for her, and followed her casket – but every day. They gathered money, gifts out of their poverty, and put beautiful windows in the church showing her likeness; and raised a chaste, gentle figure of her in their street, trodden often, at all hours, in her ministry of Love. To all, she was 'our Sister Dora'. In Walsall, during my visit, I found myself naturally recalling William Hazlitt's striking words: '*Of all eloquence,*' said he, '*a nickname is the most concise: of all arguments, the most unanswerable.*'

* * *

My first bold claim still stands: I did get through my school days and on up to adulthood, without earning for myself a nickname. But, in the most telling sense, of course, it was not so. In my teens I embraced the most wonderful nickname the world offers, although I did not know it as such at the time. It was long before I found reference to it in the New Testament, and longer still before I came upon my friend, Dr William Barclay, writing of it: 'The disciples,' he says, 'were called Christians first in Antioch' (Acts 11:26, AV). Said the doctor, underlining the significance of that historical fact: '*The word "Christian" began by being a nickname.* The people of Antioch were famous for their facility in finding jesting nicknames. Later, the bearded Emperor Julian came to visit, and they christened him "The Goat". The termination *iani* means *belonging to the party of*. For instance, Caesariani means belonging to Caesar's party, Christian means "These Christ folk". It was a half-mocking, half-jesting, wholly contemptuous nickname. But the Christians took that nickname, and made it a name not of contempt but one at the courage and love of which all men were to wonder!'

Nothing offers me richer satisfaction than strongly, eagerly to hold to that nickname today!

Good News – about Miles,
and Miles and Miles

Morning after morning, during one holiday, my friend and I slung on our haversacks, and set off through the English countryside. Spring was abroad, and the weather blessed us.

But on our twelfth day out, towards sun-down our feet began to lag. Talk between us dropped away, and each of us silently began to wonder how much farther we had to go till we came to our hostel.

At a crossroads we came upon an old man, puffing at his pipe. He seemed to be the sort of knowledgeable old soul to whom one could address a question. We told him the name of our hostel, and asked him how much farther we had to go. He answered: 'It's only another mile or two now – you'll soon be there!'

Encouraged, we stepped out brightly once more. But all too soon, we grew laggard again when no hostel came into sight. We began to wonder if he had been over-anxious to please us; or if he was, in fact, too casual to be reliable; or if, being very old, he had honestly forgotten? Eventually, we did arrive!

Our *Agreed English Mile* is derived, it seems, from the Romans' linear measurement of a thousand paces, and its name from the Latin *mille*, meaning a thousand. In time, 760 yards were added in England (and eventually wherever English people migrated), and for a very long time, our Oxford English Dictionary has accepted 1760 yards as being the measurement of our mile.

But curiously, in England there were exceptions in certain parts, as that indefatigable traveller, Celia Fiennes, recorded in her famous *Diary*. As well as *the Agreed Mile*, there was introduced *the Long Mile*. She instanced it as affecting her weary approach to Burrowbridge, now called Boroughbridge, a parish and market town of some eight hundred or so people.

'I was most sensible of the long Yorkshire miles', she wrote. In 1593, this reality must have faced many another traveller in the North by the end of the day, when even the strongest body was growing weary it could be dispiriting.

But that is not all: as well as *the Agreed Mile* and *the Long Mile* there is also *the Second Mile!* This, in the way in which we refer to it in our speech and in our daily experience, these days, is less a matter of a roadmaker's measure than a matter of spirit. And every Christian is challenged to consider it. Nowhere can you or I find its direction and distance on a fingerpost on our roadside; but there is no missing it in the teaching of our Master, Christ (Matthew 5:41, AV). 'Whosoever shall compel thee,' said He, 'to go one mile, go with him twain [two].' And all those who first heard His words knew well what He meant, for they knew the background.

Palestine was an occupied country. 'At any moment, a Jew might feel the touch of the flat of a Roman spear on his shoulder,' as Dr William Barclay reminds us in this very different day, 'and know that he was compelled to serve the Romans, it might be in the most menial way. (That, in fact, is what happened to Simon of Cyrene, when he was compelled to bear the Cross of Jesus.)'

In time, the word we render 'the Second Mile', came to mean any kind of extra service, beyond one's legal obligation. 'Sometimes,' Dr Barclay added, 'the occupying power exercised this right of compulsion in the most tyrannical and unsympathetic way . . . So then, what Jesus is saying is: "Suppose your masters come to you and compel you to be a guide or a porter for a mile, don't go a mile with bitter and obvious resentment; go *two miles* with cheerfulness and with a good grace. Don't be always thinking of your liberty to do as you like; be always thinking of your privilege to be of service to others ... A man can do the irreducible minimum and not a stroke more; he can do it in such a way that he makes it clear that he hates the whole thing ... or he can do it with a smile, with a gracious courtesy, with a determination, not only to do this thing, but to do it well ... The inefficient workman, the resentful servant, the ungracious helper has not begun to have the right idea of the Christian life."' So Dr Barclay translates the Master's words to each of us, if we are to show a truly Christian spirit, His spirit. *And it is essential for us to show the spirit Christ wants His followers to rejoice in.*

Happily, we live in a world – despite the black marks of the mass media – in which many people have caught His meaning. It is a lifting experience, over a cup of tea, or at some open gathering, to tell aloud the best example of 'the Second Mile' that one has come upon. A single memory shared can not only rejoice one's own heart, but quicken someone else to share a neighbour's, a friend's, or a stranger's right-spirited act.

Among many instances that I treasure is that of William Smyth, the doctor of medicine who practised in the Irish fishing village of Burton Port, on the coast of Donegal. *The British Medical Journal* said something unforgettable about him.

One day, news reached him that some people on a little island, about four miles off the coast, were smitten with a fever, and at once the doctor set off to row out to them. On arrival, he found that they had typhus. They had been sick for some days – too sick to go out to their fishing – and so they had no fresh food. There was no one who could help them.

Dr Smyth quickly saw what he must do, and he rowed

the four miles back to the mainland, hoping there to find helpers. But those whom he spoke with were all too afraid of the dreaded typhus. So day after day, the good doctor rowed to and fro, keeping in touch with the sick, as doctor, nurse, bedmaker, house-help, provider of food.

The idea then came that it would be best to get the very sick among them across to the hospital on the mainland. They could then have the benefit of constant skilled care. But those to whom he broke his plan felt too ill to go. Still, they trusted their doctor, and at last agreed to do whatever he proposed.

The first obstacle that faced them was where to get a boat. For the fishermen, whose livelihood depended on their boats, were loath to lend their craft, lest the fever might remain in them when the emergency was past.

Dr Smyth's own boat was far too small. But presently he found an old one abandoned in the mud. Straightway he patched it, as best he could, and got it into the water. A government inspector on the mainland, when he learned what was going on, came offering his help. A brave pair!

Together, they lay rugs in the bottom of the crazy old craft. After they had started out, it began to show a leak, and for some time it looked as if they were all to be drowned at sea. But the two fit men persevered – and rowed and rowed, and bailed and bailed in turn.

In time, they reached their landing place, and the sick with the dreaded fever were soon all in hospital. But, weakened by his protracted and tremendous effort, the doctor himself fell ill and died. When news got out to England, his fellow doctors were deeply moved, and *The British Medical Journal* inserted a wonderful tribute: 'William Smyth,' it said, 'is a glory to the whole profession, and his death in the prime of manhood must be counted more truly heroic than a death in battle . . .' He didn't stop at the 'limit of duty – he did everything humanly possible, *he truly went "the Second Mile", and gloriously'!*

One cannot live without knowing of others who, in their day-to-day life, show the same lovely spirit. And it is this for which one brings lasting thanks to our Lord!

Good News – of Horizons

I once, only once, went to a great world conference of my Church. It was in Oxford, 'city of dreaming towers and spires', and we lived, slept and worked in the old Colleges. It was vacation time, and I'll never forget it. Gracious memories were kindled there – and friendships made. I've been back several times to Oxford, although not to work, just to wander about remembering.

Chief among all who made up the fellowship of that first time was one who stood tall, so that he could not be missed in any gathering, Dr John R. Mott. I had long known his name, having read much that he had written, but had never met this valiant soul. An American by birth, a Methodist by conviction, he belonged to all the world! I had heard him called 'the world's greatest Protestant', 'the Architect of Unity'; but somebody there one day in Oxford fashioned the name that then, and ever since, has seemed to me the loveliest of all: *The Man of Horizons*.

It must have pleased him, in his quieter moments, though he made no audible response. It is a name that could well have been attributed to his beloved Master. Like Him, as a lad, John Mott had played amidst his father's timber, but in a yard to which came German, Norwegian, Finnish, Danish, Hungarian immigrant farmers for material for their barns and dwellings. Fittingly Mott's parents gave him a classroom globe, with its continents, seas and islands. He grew up to be a world citizen. There was nothing static about him.

Young John Mott served the YMCA with his early energies; then for good, full years, he was student secretary for the Student Christian Movement. Its international, interdenominational character fascinated him. One summer evening, in camp, he was one of a hundred men who volunteered for missionary service abroad. Horizons gradually opened before him – he was invited by the Librarian of Cornell University to join him in historical research in seven of the great European universities. But beforehand, he felt constrained to graduate as a Bachelor of Philosophy and Bachelor of History and Political Science.

Then, with his horizons widening even more, came his travels the world round. He remained a Methodist layman, though many thought that the Christian ministry would be his special sphere of service. The American President called him 'the world's most useful man'; in 1946 he was honoured with a half-share of the Nobel Peace Prize. And with the years, many famous universities of the world honoured him with degrees.

For thirty-one full years, John R. Mott was Chairman of the Continuation Committee of The World Missionary Conference. He was also President of the Conference in Edinburgh, in 1910; at Jerusalem, in 1928; and in Madras, in 1938. It stretches the imagination to conceive the weight of work and thought and judgement necessary in such undertakings. But he loved it – it was Life to him!

In between, somehow, he managed to write books, to edit widely-read journals, and to contribute to the press. From the start, he expected his Master to give him work to do, and as he grew, to give him ever wider and wider conceptions of His Kingdom:

> A new horizon every week;
> New hills, new sky;
> A new horizon every week
> To greet the eye.

And this, despite the fact that a considerable part of the

time during which he was fulfilling his ever-widening, creative witness, was one of great international problems – not unlike our own. Utterly dedicated to the lasting values of his Master's Kingdom, humble and sincere, men and women found it easy to bare their hearts to him, in leadership in their own area, and to love him. He was a valiant spirit in an age of far-reaching transition, a Christian who, like the earliest followers of his Master, began, as He directed them, *where they were*, in their own '*Jerusalem*', and then went on to the next horizon, to '*Judea*', then on to '*Samaria*', then on to '*the uttermost part of the earth*' (Acts 1:8, AV).

For that's how it is with horizons: always there is something more beyond – another horizon! On old Spanish coins there used to be the pillars of Hercules, and around them the motto: *Ne plus ultra*, 'nothing beyond'. But a day came – a great day – when a Genoese sailor timidly pushed his little fleet towards the horizon and, going on and on, left leagues of blue water behind him, to find before him a new world. So Spain was obliged to revise the old inscription. The pillars of Hercules were retained, but around them now were the words *plus ultra* – the *ne* omitted. Spain had found '*the beyond*'.

What that Genoese sailor did for Spain, the Master Christ, in the reality of the spirit, did for the human race: he pushed out its Horizon beyond the little local concepts they held; pushed it out beyond the limiting, distressing lines drawn between Jew and Samaritan, between barbarian and Scythian, man and woman, bond and free – pushed it out even beyond Death and the grave, representing the fears and limitations of this earthly life. His horizon reached out to the infinite and the eternal.

They hanged Him on a Cross, of course – but He rose again! He was still 'the Man of Horizons'. He led men and women, for the first time, out beyond the seen to the unseen; beyond the human to the Divine; He said: 'I tell you My friends, do not fear those who kill the body, and after that have no more that they can do' (Luke 12:4, RSV). Nor was that all. Said He, at what must have looked to those to whom He spoke as 'the last Horizon': 'Yet a little while ... *because I live, ye shall live also*' (John 14:19, AV). And those words of my Master Christ I find strangely compelling. A minister friend of mine in Canada lately set this reality in simple words for me:

> He is not dead,
> embalmed in creeds,
> wrapped in words that men can learn,
> recite, and then forget.
> *He is alive, to walk with me*
> *and with all men,*
> *to tell me of the love of God,*
> *to share with me His power,*
> *His Resurrection,*
> *and His Life!*

This was what early dawned upon John R. Mott, as a tremendous reality. And it made all the difference to everything in his life. One day, he knew quite suddenly that the resurrection of Jesus from the dead was an historic fact.

Many in our midst, alas, do not know this – and their lives are the poorer. Dr J.B. Phillips translates verses from the New Testament: 'This world is *the limit of their horizon... But our outlook goes beyond this world*' (Philippians 3:19, 20).

Acknowledgements

The author is grateful for permission to use the following material:

'When the event happened...' from *Backwards to Christmas*, J.B. Phillips; Epworth Press.
'I have heard nothing...' Poem by Ruth Gilbert.
'I had a mother...' Poem by Strickland Gillian.
Dialogue by E.J. Christoffel and lad, quoted from *Partners in Life*, edited by Geiko Muller-Fahrenholz; World Council of Churches, Geneva.
'For the first man to climb...' Poem by Lilian Cox.
'Make a space...' Poem by R.H. Grenville.
'It may be...' from *Those who Find*, Allen Birtwhistle; Epworth Press, 1951, p. 29.
'It now appears...' from *A Reason to Hope*, David L. Edwards; William Collins Sons & Co Ltd, London, 1978.
'He is not dead...' Poem by the Rev. Asa Johnson.
'Family services are immensely popular...' from the 'Demos' column of *The Methodist Recorder*, London.

The author has made every effort to trace the copyright holders of the following pieces, but without success:

'This is my Father's world...' by Maltbie Badcock, 1858–1901.
'O God our Father...' by Geoffrey Peachey.
'Measure thy life...' quoted as 'Unknown' in *Masterpieces of Religious Verse*.
'That God is...' Poem by an anonymous writer.